BENEATH MY WINGS

BENEATH MY WINGS

Rio Hogarty
with Megan Day

Hayes MacDermot Publishing

Published by Hayes MacDermot
Unit 11, Woodview Court,
Tandy's Lane,
Lucan,
Co Dublin,
Ireland.
www.irishbooksandauthors.com

First published, 2011

A CIP record for this book is available from the British Library

ISBN 978-0-9563598-8-9

While the stories included in this book are true, names, locations and dates
have been changed to protect the identities of other people, including many
of the children Rio has helped throughout her life. Any resemblance to
persons, living or dead, is purely coincidental.

Printed in Ireland with Print Procedure Ltd.
Typesetting: Paul McElheron. Cover Design: Jessica Maile.
Photographs: Rio Hogarty's personal collection.
Front cover image: Getty Images.
Back cover images: Sportsfile, Ger Woods.

Contents

Photographs

Foreword

Rio Hogarty is an extraordinary woman – warm hearted but tough as nails, ordinary yet extraordinary. Rio is one of those inspiring people who, as soon as you meet them, impress you. There are the obvious reasons; her charisma, her humour, her good nature, but it goes deeper than that – it's her ability to accept people as they are and empower them to achieve their potential, that is what makes Rio extraordinary.

Rio has seen it all, nothing shocks her any more. She has 'trucked' her way across Europe, hemmed many a dress and helped hundreds of people get back on their feet – and that's not counting the 140 children she has welcomed into her home. For many of those children, being fostered by Rio was a life-changing experience. She provided opportunities to children who may never have otherwise had them.

Today, she is a full-time care giver to the four children in her home, an avid gardener, a formidable campaigner and a seasoned singer on the stage – Rio seems to have time for everything and for everyone.

She is eternally popular in the tight-knit community of Clondalkin. Her can-do attitude is simply infectious, but she cushions it well with realism. She is acutely aware of the challenges people face and does far more than empathise with them, she rolls up her sleeves and helps them turn things around. Her grit and determination mean that she never gives up on anyone or any cause. She is the type of person who, when confronted with a 'no', asks 'why not?'

Rio says that, no matter where she is, she can close her eyes and say a prayer to the angels and then everything will be ok, but, for so many, it's Rio who is the real guardian angel.

She will tell you she is ordinary, but Rio's tremendous ability to accept people for who they are, to motivate others to achieve their goals and her infectious, positive personality have made her a real inspiration.

In many ways, she has had an extraordinary life, but really, Rio is right, this is the story of an ordinary person; an ordinary person who has done extraordinary things.

This is Rio's story.

Frances Fitzgerald, TD
Minister for Children and Youth Affairs

Preface

In September 2010, RTÉ – in partnership with Quinn Healthcare and Rehab – gave out their annual People of the Year Awards at a lavish, televised ceremony.

It was a stellar year, with an impressive array of recipients ranging from a young man who swam the English Channel to medical workers who assisted in the aftermath of the Haiti hurricane. Amongst them was a winner in a new category, one that had been designed that year specifically for the extraordinary woman who would be the recipient. For the first time in its history, there was an award for the Mother of the Year. It was given to a seventy-three-year-old woman named Rio Hogarty, who had raised two of her own children and then helped to raise one hundred and forty more who could not be raised by their own parents.

This would be a remarkable accomplishment for anyone, at any time. But it is merely one aspect of a life that has brimmed full with hardship, achievement and a great deal of tough love. Raised in working-class Dublin during the Depression and post-war years, Rio had a childhood that managed to be magical, exciting and loving. A tomboy at heart, she was always the champion of the smaller or more timid children in her neighbourhood. A natural but unassuming leader, she always fought for the underdog, whether it was a school friend with a brutal, alcoholic father or a seven-year-old street urchin abandoned to survive on the streets.

The stories associated with the scores of children Rio has helped over the years are many and varied, but at the centre of them all is the pivotal story of the woman who has dedicated herself to others, so selflessly, for so many decades.

What kind of person does such a thing? And where does she come from?

This book is not the story – or the many stories – of the children in her care. This is the story of how a heart so big came into being in the first place, of how the little girl with scabby knees from south Dublin became the indomitable woman with the strength to gather so many broken hearts and give them the wings to fly.

This is the story of Rio Hogarty.

Introduction

Magic and magical. That is how I describe my childhood. Running barefoot through the fields of south Dublin to pick blackberries, climbing recklessly into the high branches of the tallest trees, peering with a wide-eyed fascination into the fairy rings of mushroom caps in the squelchy ground of the garden, surrounded by love and lore and adventure.

I guess because people now know me for what turned out to be my life's calling, they think I must have been drawn to it due to a trauma or want in my own childhood. It is assumed, I think, that I must have been a wounded child myself, to be so dedicated to tending to the wounds of others. But this is not the case – my childhood was happy, enchanted even.

So, when people ask me why I did what I have done, they are expecting me to say that I shared some understanding of pain and loss and could, therefore, identify with it: Not at all. I loved being a child and, while my sisters couldn't wait to wear high heels and lipstick and be all 'grown up', I hung on to the freedoms and fascinations of my youth like a clinging vine and would happily have never let go. It was a shock to me to learn that there were young people suffering during what should have been the most carefree and glorious years of their lives. I had thought life was magical for everyone.

What I have always wanted is for every youngster to experience at least some of the magic that enthralled me as a child. I wanted to share it and, in some small way, with every child that has been under my roof over the last forty years, I have tried to bring that feeling of magical freedom into their lives – and, at the same time, to relive a bit of that magic for myself.

So, this is the story of my childhood and early years, the framework, I suppose, onto which I built the skills that later served me so well. If I have succeeded in some small way in helping others, it is because the friends and family and loved ones, of all shapes, sizes and forms, that came and went throughout my life gave me the strength, the courage and the desire to spread my wings.

Rio Hogarty
Clondalkin, Ireland
February, 2011

Acknowledgments

This book is dedicated to all the children who have come and gone in my life. Thank you for the happy times, thank you also for the sad times. I wouldn't have missed a minute of it. May you have all the best of everything in the many years ahead of you.

Thanks also to the special people in my life. To Pat Whelan – I could not have gotten through my life without her help – she was the guardian angel beneath my wings. To Sylvia Godfrey who was my lifelong friend. And to Helen Power and Saundra Martin, my right and left hands for nearly fifteen years – we proved that three women can work in the same kitchen! And also to Aiden Waterstone, Mary Cummins, Annette O'Malley, and all of the staff at the Irish Foster Care Association office. And not to forget Sid Gannon, who always wanted to write a book about our escapades but went on to the big escapade in the sky before he got the chance.

Last, but never least, thanks to my own family – to my long-suffering husband and all of my loved ones. We all got through this together.

Rio Hogarty

Author's Note

All of the stories in this book are true.

Now, having said that, I have to qualify and add that although the things that Rio did and the things that happened to Rio are true, we did have to change names and places and sometimes dates in order to protect the identities of others. Some of these are the children whom Rio helped and, obviously, their privacy is paramount. Others are adults who may – or may not – want to be identified and, rather than err on the side of infringing on someone's right to be anonymous if they so choose, we opted to obscure the identities of just about everybody.

There are loads of people out there who know Rio and who have been part of her life. If you are reading this book and thinking, "That person in that story may be me!", all I can say is – no, it's not.

Just relax, read and enjoy the story of this extraordinary woman because that is what this book is really about – it's about her.

Megan Day
County Kildare, Ireland
2011

Prologue

South Dublin, 1948

Rio tied one end of the string to the chicken's leg and the other end to the tree.

The chicken (whom Brother Brown had named Flora) was accustomed to being handled – pampered even – and other than being a bit restless while she had been in the feed sack, she had been calm. And expectant. Flora knew that whenever she spent much time with people, she got some delicious treats.

When Rio threw plain old corn on the ground in front of her, she blinked as well as a chicken can and waited to see if something better might be on offer.

Rio stayed crouched on the ground, looking at Flora – while Flora politely looked back – and frowned.

So far, all had gone well.

Dominic, Jane and Brian were tying up the other three chickens. Dominic's was less cooperative and started to squawk. They might as well have set off an air-raid siren, it seemed so loud – surely that incessant screeching was a beacon that would announce their crime to the whole world.

Shit.

She jumped up, abandoned Flora and ran over to Dominic who had put his arms over his head as he cowered on the ground and let the irate chicken (Brother Brown called this speckled beauty, Dora) beat at him with her whipping flurry of wings.

Rio scooped Dora up and soothed her.

"Now, now," she said and pulled a handful of corn out of her pocket. Dora wasn't any more thrilled with such a mundane treat than Flora had been, but allowed herself to be mollified.

The squawking stopped, at any rate.

Rio put her on the ground and let her peck at the corn in a way that clearly conveyed she found it only mildly satisfying. The string around Dora's leg dragged on the ground. None of the chickens had been too interested in seeing how far they could get from the tree – or the corn.

Jane was handling it well. She had been scared of the chickens at first. Her little hands had shaken when they gave her a writhing sack full of furious feathers. Carmen was the name of the precious hen she had carried – Brother Brown thought it would be disrespectful to name the chickens after saints, also he had a definite but, in his mind, wholesome fascination with film stars.

Scratching feet and sharp beaks aside, Jane had wanted to help her big brother. Brother Brown had been horrible to Dominic. Always shouting, scolding and boxing his ears. When, after a particularly brutal episode, Rio had suggested it was time to teach Brother Brown a lesson, it had not taken much convincing. Not for any of them.

And now, part one of the plan was done.

Brother Brown's prize chickens – French Mottled Houdans, to be precise – were lovely, with their white plumage speckled with black and white spots and the impressive, flouncy crests on their heads. As they promenaded around the tree they looked like a bevy of well-heeled matrons with their Sunday-best bouncing bonnets. Yes, they were lovely.

Dominic dusted off his knees and stepped out of Dora's range, though she pointedly ignored him. Brian, who had made fast friends with his cargo, named Vivienne, threw a handful of corn at Dominic.

It smacked against his bare knee like gravel.

"Ow!"

Brian and Rio both sniggered, though Rio also patted his shoulder.

"Ah, you're all right now."

Dominic shrugged his shoulder away.

"Yeah, yeah. So, now what?"

They all watched the chickens for a few minutes as they contentedly continued pecking at the ground, only occasionally twitching the leg that had the string attached to it, as if it were a bracelet that didn't fit properly.

"They seem happy, don't they?" Jane wasn't sure how to tell if chickens were happy, but she thought that quietly pecking at the ground and not trying to beat the bejesus out of her brother might be a hint of some form of happiness.

"Yes, we just need to give them some water and they'll be grand."

Rio spoke, as usual, with authority. She had learned, somewhere way back in the entire twelve years of her life, that if you sound like you know what you're talking about, it's generally almost as good as actually knowing.

Brian pulled a small tin bowl out of his satchel and a small milk bottle that no longer contained milk.

"Here we are – here's the water and bowl and all."

"Okay, so." Rio knelt and cleared a spot where the chickens would be able to reach the bowl and, hopefully, not knock it over with their strings – but they might. One thing she did know about chickens was that they were pretty stupid. She would need to come out here often and make sure the water dish was kept full.

Once the spare corn feed was stashed in a nearby bush that the chickens couldn't reach, it was time to pack up the sacks into Brian's satchel and head back.

The sun was starting to set, the leafy shadows in the woods were lengthening and the light came down awkwardly, at a lazy slant.

The four of them headed back towards the farm – the next part of the plan was to put the feed sacks back where they had found them. Rio had thought about that part – if the sacks were missing, everyone at the farm would know it was an 'inside job'. She had heard her da use that phrase once when he was talking about a bank robbery that had been reported in the newspaper. Even then, she had known that if she ever had to do something that other people didn't need to know about, she wouldn't be so sloppy as to leave telltale signs. She was thorough.

If Brother Brown was to be properly chastised for his ill-treatment of Dominic and the other boys, he had to fear more than just the petty pranks of the kids who helped at the rectory farm – he had to fear punishment that could come from anywhere, at any time.

He had to fear the very hand of God.

Once they got back to the periphery of the farmyard, they stopped, hidden behind the prickly hedge. They peered through the foliage and made sure the place was empty. It was dusk, nearly dark, and everything was silent except for the shuffling and snorting of the mules and cows in the barn on the opposite side of the yard.

The grain shed was so close they could almost touch it. Someone just had to break cover and dash through the shed door and leave the feed sacks on the shelf where they had found them.

Brian wasn't a bit afraid. He gave Rio a nod and made his dash.

The other three held their breaths for the two minutes it took him to toss the sacks into the shed and race back to them. He had not made sure that the sacks were stacked neatly back on the shelf. This worried Rio.

It was not the sort of detail she would have overlooked but, bless him, Brian had been brave enough to run in and do it, so they would have to hope it was good enough.

Brian was breathless when he got back to the hedge – perhaps he had been holding his breath as well.

"Done and dusted!"

"Very good." Rio was back in charge. "Now we can head home but, remember, we have to take the long way so they won't see us coming from here. They can't know we were anywhere near the chickens today."

And with that they were off, back into the woods and then looping a wide berth around the farm building, in the direction of the chapel.

They made a wide berth around that as well. Jane couldn't help but wonder if it was a mortal or a venal sin to steal someone's prize chickens – even if it wasn't really 'stealing', according to Rio, who claimed it was a complicated sort of borrowing without permission but for a good reason that was for the betterment of Brother Brown's soul. Jane hadn't learned all her catechism yet, but she feared she was on shaky moral ground here, no matter how much she felt Brother Brown deserved it.

The woods were now pitch black and it was a relief to see the twinkling lights of the chapel in the distance and to see the small road ahead that would lead back home.

They were tired but laughing as they realised they had actually succeeded in their Brilliant Plan. Brian had done a very commendable impersonation of Dora – or perhaps Flora – flapping wings and bobbing head and disdainful looks included. They had just finished squealing and snorting, laughing and jostling along the path when a blaze of light burst into their faces and paralysed them with its holy glare.

A voice rose over the mesmerising beams.

"Children? What are you doing here this time of night?"

It was Father O'Dowd. There was no mistaking that voice. The light from the torch in his hand bobbed a minute, then settled somewhere around their knees as he came closer.

As he towered over them, the four thieving children gazed up, beatifically, into his face, subsumed in a silence that, to Rio, seemed to throb with guilt.

"Well? What are you children doing out this way at this time of the night?"

Rio's normally glib tongue was stuck like a swollen melon in her mouth – she worked her lips, ground her teeth, trying to force a slippery story into the space between them.

Shockingly, it was Jane who spoke up. Tiny Jane with her trembling voice, teardrops edging her wispy eyelashes.

"Oh, Father – we were just at the chapel."

Rio's head nearly snapped off her neck as she swung around to look at her clearly underestimated compatriot. *Brilliant*, she thought – *and why did I not think of it?*

"The chapel? Whatever would you four need to be going to chapel for at this time of night?"

Well, Jane had started it so Rio let her run with it.

But instead of a credible, if somewhat cheesy, story escaping her tender lips, Jane broke into a near hysterical sob, crushed under the weight of impending Catholic guilt.

"Oh, Father! We have done something terrible."

A thunderous silence followed.

And, for the second time that day, Rio thought to herself, *Shit*. Father O'Dowd towered over them quietly for a moment. The only sound was the sniffing still coming from Jane.

Rio didn't know where to look. She decided to focus on Father O'Dowd's hand that was holding the flashlight. She assumed it was the same hand that would reach out and grab them all by the hair and drag them to be presented as lying thieves to their parents, so it would be good to keep an eye on that hand.

"What exactly is this terrible thing?" Father O'Dowd's voice had that quiet quality that people with ferocious tempers often have.

Again, Rio tried to work a mealy-mouthed lie out of her mouth. Anything. Anything at all would do, any sort of nonsense that was far removed from chickens. Once again, she found her tongue frozen and lumpish, clogging any transmissions coming from her beleaguered brain to her vocal chords. Once again, it was Jane who spoke up.

"None of us had been to confession this week, Father. We are taking the long way home as a penance."

Her sobbing became very believable, if somewhat overwrought, at this point. The flashlight flickered across their faces. Truly, they looked like the most pathetically guilty and repentant group of little buggers he had ever seen. It was a miracle.

"Alright then. It is getting late and your parents will be worried. Off you go."

As they made an impressively rapid escape, Rio's estimation of Jane increased by a factor of several million.

The next morning, Brother Brown discovered his missing chickens and raised alarms all over the parish. His hysteria was frightening, and very satisfactory. The children dutifully helped, along with everyone else, to comb the area near the rectory farm, and Brother Brown was touched to notice that, in their concern, they volunteered to scour the distant woods as well. Although they reported that they had found nothing.

The police were brought in and Brother Brown had to berate them in beetroot-faced rage, for not being more energetic about solving the 'major crime' that had occurred on rectory property. He blamed their city upbringing when they suggested that perhaps the chickens had just 'wandered off'.

Brother Brown remained bereft, heartbroken and prickly with anger as the searching produced no sign of his prized flock. It was, therefore, quite baffling when, two mornings after they disappeared, as he made his usual rounds in the farmyard to collect the average eggs that were laid by the average hens, that he heard some heart-stoppingly familiar cackling.

And there they were.

Dora, Flora, Carmen and Vivienne were promenading in their enclosure, as haughty and bright-eyed as the day they had left.

No one ever came forward to claim responsibility, no one ever proposed a logical motive and the police officers that Brother Brown spent so much time trying to brow-beat into obedience, never solved the crime.

But Brother Brown did change after the experience. Something in his nature shifted, some inkling in his soul suspected that perhaps the Lord was not entirely pleased with him and had sent this affliction, this poultry purgatory, in order that he might examine where he was lacking in holy wholesomeness. He actually became a slightly kinder man.

A few days after all the excitement had blown over, Rio was walking to the farm with her granddad.

"Funny thing," he said. "No one remarked on it, but I couldn't help but notice that a couple of Brother Brown's hens had corn grains in their feathers."

"Really?" Rio adopted what she thought was an innocent expression.

"And, stranger still, there were some chicken feathers in a couple of the feed sacks. White feathers, with black spots."

Rio said nothing and looked away in case the innocence had slipped off her face. They continued walking, with neither of them speaking. In fact, Granddad never mentioned it again. But he smiled whenever he saw those lovely, arrogant hens parading in their special chicken yard, each of them shaking one leg as if it had a string attached.

Part One

Magic and Magical

I realise now, looking back, that from the day I came into the world, I was not what anyone expected me to be. I was not the son my da had been hoping for as a first-born; and my skinned knees and wild ways as I was growing up meant that I was never the precious little lady that my mam had wanted. But while their expectations were still intact, they had given me a lovely, lyrical name - Rita Mary O'Reilly. Yet, even that did not turn out as planned.

Before long, my da was calling me Richeen - his little Richeen. And hearing it so often, I came to believe Richeen was my proper name. So, on my first day of school, when the gaggle of children wanted to know what I was called, I was surprised to find that 'Richeen' did not roll easily off the tongues of five-year-olds.

"Reechy?"

Absolutely not.

"Reetsie?"

"No," I insisted, "it's Richeen."

My new friend, Mary, was particularly unimpressed.

"I don't like it", she sniffed. After only a moment she insisted, "I like Rio better."

And I guess I did, too, because I have been Rio ever since. Well, I was always Richeen to my da, of course. Always.

Having a different name suited my temperament which was, according to my da, 'spirited' and, according to my ma, 'difficult'. In my mind, it was also a name that meant I didn't have to be treated like a girl, or act like one. Tree climbing, running barefoot through the fields, scaling walls and jumping off them – my mother thought that a girl wearing a skirt wouldn't do such things. She was wrong.

I suppose it is only now, looking back, that I realise the tension this perhaps caused between my parents – my da loving my boyish attitude, my mother despairing of it. At the time, I only felt loved by the two most important people in my life, one with complete acceptance and the other with a sort of reluctant chagrin, but love me they did.

And that bedrock of love was the ground from which I launched myself from one adventure to another. Like a puppy who had never known a collar and lead, I followed my nose and my curiosity wherever it led me.

My grandfather introduced me to the hidden magical world right in my own back garden. He told me all about the faerie folk living in the greenery. I knew of their kingdoms and domains, their music, their legendary feasts and their charms that could beguile humans.

Oh, how I wanted to be beguiled.

We would spend hours exploring the garden for signs of the wee ones, and put our ears to the ground listening for the telltale signs of their revelries. In the early morning, following a rainy night, we would hunt for the rings of uprising mushrooms, a sure sign that they had favoured our garden as a location for one of their magical cities. I never doubted they were there for a minute. In many ways, even today, I still do not doubt them. There was never anything about nature that frightened or intimidated me, which was not a sign of bravery but more a pig-headed belief in my own immortality.

One winter that was abnormally frigid, my mother had bought me a lovely new coat, hat and gloves. I was not immune to the idea of looking like a girl, I wore my new attire proudly and was quite delighted with myself. But when Peggy, Mary and I were walking across the rectory grounds – a favourite place to play – the frozen fish-pond was too fascinating to resist.

Instead of the usual rippling, slightly scummy surface with flashes of the darting, large gold carp below, all we could see was a crusty flatness, dusted with snow.

"Jaysus, the goldfish must be frozen!" Mary was somewhere between terrified and morbidly fascinated.

"Wouldn't they be able to live under the ice? Couldn't they keep themselves warm and find things to eat under there?" Peggy was always a bit more practical.

"Let's go and see." That, of course, was me. I was never good with theory.

We walked to the very edge between the frozen grass and the forlorn, stiff stalks of reed that bordered the water. We peered down, fully expecting to see the solid bodies of the goldfish embedded in the ice like pebbles. Instead, we couldn't see much of anything. I poked my booted foot onto the ice.

"It seems really solid." As if I knew. Oh, well.

Ever practical, Peggy came up with a good plan.

"I bet we could run all the way across."

Now there was an amazing possibility – running across a pond! My feet tingled at the idea of skimming across the surface where, during the summer, we had thrown breadcrumbs that had bobbed languidly until gulped by the overfed goldfish.

"Yes, I think we could!"

"Alright, here I go." And then Peggy was off, dashing across the ten-foot width of the pond about as quickly as an eight-year-old girl in a bulky coat and clunky boots can dash.

She got to the other side, turned around and jumped up and down a little bit.

"Come on! Come on!"

Mary made her mad dash. There was an alarming cracking sound just before she reached the other side, but she was grinning as she bounced up and down next to Peggy.

"Come on! Come on!" They were both shouting now.

I started across. Somewhere in the middle, it occurred to me that we had still not solved the puzzle of what had happened to the fish. I stopped and looked down. I realised that I could see a difference in the colour of the ice here, that there was an edge to the chalky part I was standing on and the darker bit below ... that was water.

"Hey!", I called out. "There *is* water under there! The fish must be swimming around below the ice!"

I bent over, scanning the watery layers below me, looking for a sign of our gold, scaly friends.

There was another alarming crack.

"What's that?" Mary looked back towards the rectory buildings. To be fair, we had never stood on ice before. We didn't know what the cracking meant or where it came from.

Then I noticed the marks in the ice. It was as if I was suddenly in the middle of a spider's web constructed from shards of glass. Then the solidness beneath me shifted.

I don't remember making any sound. Peggy and Mary insist that I hollered like a banshee, but then they would since they got to stay dry and watch me crash through the slivers of ice and plop like a rock down to the bottom of the pond.

I suppose it should have been the shock of the cold that got to me, but that's not what I remember. It was the falling ... down and down until my feet hit the bottom. Instinctively, I just pushed against the gooey solidness and propelled myself up to the surface.

The water was only barely over my head. Peggy and Mary were watching with eyes as goggled as the goldfish's when I spluttered to the surface. The ice around me had crackled into smithereens and I was able to work my way over to where the water was shallower.

With my feet firmly planted and my head above water, I walked out of the pond and stood, dripping, next to the girls.

It seemed suddenly silent, then I realised that Mary and Peggy had been screaming at me up until that moment. Really useful advice, I think – things like, "Get out of there, Rio!", "Don't drown!", "Come over this way!" And the terrifying, "Your ma is gonna kill you!"

In spite of that last sobering remark, as we all stood there, the two of them warm and dry and me dripping and with bits of greenish slime clinging to me, we couldn't help it, we went from giggling to laughing ourselves sick in thirty seconds flat.

All the way home, in spite of my chattering teeth, we laughed and re-lived the adventure. It became epic in the retelling – an adventure on the arctic tundra full of frozen treachery and giggling schoolgirls.

When I got home, I was still laughing about it and ran in to tell my ma.

"Ma! Ma! Guess what happened!"

Oops. Her icy response was more chilling than a plunge in a frozen fish-pond – and I should know.

All I could think of was the adventure of it, the hilarity, the surprise. All she could see was my new coat, soaked and slimy.

I was stripped out of my freezing wet clothes, a hot bath was prepared and the new coat, hat and gloves were taken away to be cleaned and dried: I think they all recovered nicely, but I don't know for sure because the next time I went out, I was given my old coat – I never saw my lovely new one again.

My mother made me promise that my reckless tomboy days were over after the frozen pond incident.

She had sensed, as mothers do, that I felt the loss of my lovely new coat rather keenly. This, she assumed, was a sign that I was turning a corner.

For the next couple of weeks I kept to my promise. I refused to be drawn into climbing over garden walls if I could walk around them; I resisted crawling on my stomach in the mud even though I knew it would have gotten me into the best hiding place *ever* for hide and seek; I turned down the dare to see how hard my fountain pen had to be squeezed before the ink would squirt out the sides instead of the tip (that was a tough one – I was dying to see how that went).

But I had forgotten about the tree. No one could say no to the tree.

Just inside the gate to the Holy Ghost Fathers' church and rectory, there was a massive, majestic oak tree that appeared to be about the same age as God. The trunk was as big around as a car and it was nearly as tall as the church spire. Best of all, its limbs were thick, the bottom ones fairly low to the ground, and the progression of their leafy arms staggered upward in an inviting array somewhere between a ladder and a staircase.

The way the branches bunched together in places, with knobbly galls like handholds in between, was a tree climber's dream. To us, it was as if Jesus had placed the tree on his holy ground as an example of what the perfect climbing tree should be.

The challenge, of course, was to discover how high one could climb it. The record was currently held by Dominic, who had reached a point level with the top of the stained glass window over the church door. Some were convinced that this record would never be broken.

You see, it was not just a matter of climbing the tree. Given its majestic symmetry, climbing was easy. The problem was the priests.

Knowing an irresistible temptation when they saw one, the priests had very strictly forbidden us from climbing the tree. Ever. Which had exactly the effect you would expect – we had devised ways of climbing the tree when the priests weren't looking.

The trick was for a few of us to gather under the tree with our book satchels and to sit on the grass, under the leafy boughs, with books in hand as if we were studying. The kids with the books were, in fact, the lookouts.

While one intrepid climber began their ascent, the ones with the books had the job of shouting a signal when a priest was seen anywhere nearby. The usual alarm was to yell, "Look at this!" very loudly while pointing at something in the book. Whoever was up in the tree then knew to come to a complete standstill and not draw any attention to themselves. When the priest was out of view, the all-clear was given and climbing could continue.

The Great Tree Climbing Challenge was not planned. Like many pivotal moments in one's history, it was completely spontaneous. On an unusually mild day in late winter, the gang of us were walking past the tree and the gauntlet was thrown.

Perhaps it was a blessing, perhaps it was a curse, but I was a great tree climber. Shifting myself from branch to branch was almost as effortless as walking. Peggy, rather dismissively, accused me of being part monkey but, regardless of whether it was a good thing or not, it was a talent nonetheless. And, when Brian O'Donnelly told me that no one would ever climb higher than Dominic, I could not let it stand. Not so much because of my ego but because it was simply an untruth. Left unbothered by pesky disciplinarians, I knew I could climb all the way to the very top of that tree.

So, with lookouts in place, books in their hands, I started my climb.

The first leg was the only part that could not be climbed alone. The bottom-most low-hanging branch was just beyond our grasp, so, with Brian and Peggy standing on some stacked satchels and hoisting me with linked hands, I was propelled to my launching point for the big climb.

Hand over hand, swinging one leg at a time over tree limb after tree limb, it was going well. I had just reached a particularly large, broad branch that was always the first stopping point when I heard the alarm. I scooted as close as I could to the trunk and held my breath.

My enforced rest was short – it was just a priest hurrying past, so, within moments I was back on the climb.

I am not particularly fearful of heights but then I'm not crazy, I have a healthy respect for gravity, and I knew that looking down could make me dizzy. So I kept my head up and continued to just climb and climb. Shouts of encouragement floated up on occasion. As well as hoots that were meant to distract me – apparently Dominic had showed up and wanted to make sure that his record was secure.

I had a couple of minor close calls – scraped my knee, grazed my knuckles, got smacked across the eyes by a whippy branch. But I slogged on, always looking above me, always searching for that next handhold.

As I pulled myself up onto one particularly knobbly branch I heard a commotion from below. It wasn't the usual alarm.

"Take a look from where you are!" It was Peggy.

Then I heard other voices. "It's the window! It's the window!"

I looked towards the front of the church and, sure enough, I was level with the stained glass window. I was almost to the high mark that Dominic had set. I looked down for a moment to wave to them.

Whoa!

I started to sway a little bit as the shock of their seemingly tiny faces hit me. I turned away to look at the stained glass again. That was better. Feeling a bit shaken, but no less determined, I reached above me to a medium-sized branch which, if I swung on it slightly, could propel me to a bigger branch a little higher and to the right of the branch I was on. I had just started the swing when I heard the alarm.

"Look at this!" came wafting up to me in a high-pitched chorus that sounded more urgent than usual.

I flailed my legs towards the bigger branch, but it was slick with dead, brown leaves and I got no footing. Instead I swung back and forth, finally coming to a standstill with nothing beneath my feet at all.

I hung there motionless for a moment, knowing I did not want to make any kind of sound or movement that would make a priest look up. I waited for the all-clear, picturing in my mind the priest scurrying past the gate, oblivious to the anxious children with their upside down school books. As soon as he was gone, I would get the signal.

So, I waited.

My arms started to tremble. I didn't want to swing again

towards the branch – it might make too much noise or the movement might be so large that it would catch someone's eye. Feeling my fingers getting slippery, I dug the toes of my shoes into the bark of the tree trunk, trying to take some weight off my arms. That helped. For a few minutes.

Still no all-clear.

Now my legs and my arms were shaking. What on earth was going on down there? I managed to get one hand loose and grabbed onto a thicker branch to my left, heading back to the hefty limb I had been standing on before. I grabbed hold of it and tried to swing my leg over the bigger branch. My leg got over and the small branch slipped from my hand, throwing me off balance. With one leg over the big limb and one hand still on the larger branch, I managed to slip around and end up hanging nearly upside down, with one arm and leg flapping uselessly among the dead leaves. A tiny loose twig fluttered down to the ground. I gasped and turned my attention to the wavering earth below me, expecting to see the accusing glare of a priest blazing back at me.

But there was no priest. That was good. But there was no one else either. Everyone was gone. Not even a satchel in sight.

Bugger.

As I wobbled in the air, trying to make sense of my situation, the colours of the stained glass window off to my right caught my eye. I was so close. And I knew that there was a lovely set of branches above my head leading like a staircase to well above the apex of the window. I was going to do this.

At least I didn't have to worry about making noise, so off I went, swinging myself upright and hoisting myself to the next set of branches, scrabbling up by handholds on the shallow ledges of ancient grooves and folds in the bark of the tree trunk. My hair got caught on one particularly spindly branch and, as I pushed myself past it, a clump of curly hair stuck, waving in the small puffs of breezy air.

Onward and upward, with no looking down and no niggling worries about holes torn in the knees of my tights, I just kept climbing.

The air around me suddenly seemed quite still, the creaking of the branches was the only thing I could hear. And then I realised – I had no more branches above me big enough to climb on. The next six feet or so tapered off over my head, the thin, wispy branches hanging onto clumps of dead leaves with cranky tenacity.

As far as climbing went, I had reached the top. I looked out around me, I could see into the opening in the spire where the bell hung. All my life I had heard that bell ring – on Sundays, on holy days, for weddings, funerals and christenings – but I had never seen it.

It had bird poop on it.

It now dawned on me that at this pinnacle of my tree-climbing career, no one was there to see me. And no one – especially Dominic – would ever believe what I had done.

I sat in a very unladylike way on the last branch that would support me and searched through my coat pockets. Among the used bus tickets, sweet wrappers and petrified chewing gum, I managed to find a bottle cap. I applied the sharp edge to the bark and scraped some shallow markings that looked more or less like an 'R' and an 'O'. Rio O'Reilly had been here.

I spat on my fingers and wiped the initials clean. There. Now it was time for the descent. For the first time since I had reached the top, I looked straight down.

Bugger.

I had to close my eyes and hold onto the trunk very tightly for a few seconds. After that, I would only look down as far as my next foothold. This was no time to get dizzy.

The climb down took nearly as long as the climb up. Without my lookouts below, I was hesitant to go too fast or to make too much noise. At last I made it to the bottom-most branch. I looked around, hoping someone had come back. I was now cold, hungry and tired and decided I would have to find a way to get down by myself. After what I had just done, it seemed like it wasn't an unreasonable challenge.

I tried some exploratory scraping with my foot to see if the bark might be uneven enough to give me a foothold. It was a bit dodgy – slippery in some places, rough and creased in others, giving a promise of providing some traction. I decided to risk it and slipped off the branch, hanging by my hands, scrabbling with my feet until I was stuck in. Now I had to see if there were any small branches or large bumps where I could get a hand-hold.

It was then that I heard a voice that nearly made me jump out of my skin.

"What are you doing there?"

The voice was behind me, there was no mistaking Father O'Dowd.

He continued. "I sent all you children off half an hour ago. Now, get down off that tree."

I was hanging slightly above his head. It was not clear to me how he expected me to cover the distance. Perhaps he thought I would sprout wings and just flutter down in an angelic cloud. Instead, I panicked and tried to grab the tree trunk with my hands, keeping my toes dug in. This had rather the opposite effect of an angelic fluttering.

I smacked the bottom of my chin squarely on the branch and then landed bumpily near Father O'Dowd's feet, wheezing from having the wind knocked out of me. He reached down and pulled me to my feet. I gulped as I felt a trickle from my chin down my neck. I swiped at it with my sleeve.

"You're alright now, aren't you?" Father O'Dowd looked at me with an expression that just *dared* me to say otherwise.

I just nodded, not sure what might come out of my mouth. It seemed like a scream had curled up on my tongue and was waiting to jump out. I didn't dare give it a chance.

Without another word, I ran off leaving Father O'Dowd and my initials behind.

It wasn't until twelve years later, when they closed the Holy Fathers' church and rectory and started building flats, that the tree was cut down. I could have proven to my friends then, once and for all, that I had reached the top. But, of course, no one was around any more who would have cared.

My mother knew I had climbed it, though. Well, she knew I had done something. The torn stockings, scraped knuckles, scratched face and filthy shoes were pretty damning evidence. The kind I could usually explain away, though. But there was no getting around the skin scraped off the bottom of my chin...

⁂

The end of the summer meant blackberries.

Gangs of us would go out, with baskets and pillow cases, to collect whatever we couldn't eat from the masses of bushes that grew all around the edges of the fields.

We were in the city, but the semi-wild fields lay crouched around us like old sleeping cats, knowing their days were numbered.

One day, I was out with my usual crowd to pick berries. At the ripe old age of ten, most of them were younger than me and needed some minding.

Derek still had a hard time distinguishing ripe berries from green ones. He didn't think colour should be the deciding factor. In his mind, if he could reach it, then it was a berry that should be picked. And eaten. He even ate one that had a caterpillar on it. He would cry and blubber and be unable somehow to actually spit it out. Derek later grew to be a strapping, big fellow. I think he may owe it all to eating caterpillars.

Little Jane was constantly getting snagged by the blackberry briars. Sometimes it was her hair, and she would shriek. Sometimes it was her clothes, and she would cry. Whenever she got a scratch on her hand, it was a major catastrophe with shrieking and crying and all berry picking had to stop while I tended to her wounds.

Mary, Peggy and Katie were under strict orders from their mothers to bring home enough berries to make a pie. Unfortunately, none of them were clear on exactly how many berries that might be. Peggy had a theory she was trying out that meant for every berry she ate, she should put two in the basket. As the morning went on, that seemed exorbitant and she opted for a one-to-one ratio.

It was warm that day but not hot, so it did not seem odd to see a fellow in a raincoat approaching.

We all noticed him, as he followed the hedge from the far side of the field over to where we were. I couldn't say I knew him, but he looked a bit familiar, like he had a resemblance to someone I perhaps knew.

The first thing about him that was wrong was that he was so much older than us. Berry picking was a task for us kids. And, anyway, he didn't even have a basket or anything.

When I mentioned this, Peggy suggested that his coat pockets would probably suffice. Well, if that was the case, he certainly wasn't planning on making a pie. We carried on with our picking.

Jane had caught her stocking on some nettles. This created a whole new level of panic, which was apparently so heightened it actually prevented her from shrieking. It required careful manoeuvring just the same, to extricate the ankle without getting her snagged by either more nettles or some briars. By the time I got her loose, my left hand was on fire with nettle stings and a briar had scratched me just below my eye.

So, there we were with Jane freed and only whimpering, Derek making headway with some berries that he could reach that were only slightly tinged with green, the other girls accumulating enough uneaten berries to at least make a substantial tart and I was rubbing dew-drenched grass into the nettle-inflamed area of my hand when we heard the footsteps behind us.

Out of the corner of my eye, I saw the quizzical look on Peggy's ever-so-logical face. I turned and saw our visitor. The man in the raincoat.

At the time, I thought he was ancient. My guess was that he was at least twenty-two. In my mind, the difference between twenty-two and eighty-seven was rather indistinct.

At any rate, he was not one of us and not someone I knew. I wasn't frightened, just curious.

At first, he just stood there. The kids continued picking berries and our visitor seemed unsure what to do next. He was fumbling strangely with both hands in his raincoat pockets. Between the tops of his unlaced boots and the hem of his poorly fitting coat, I noticed a glimpse of hairy leg.

My first thought was that everyone knows you should have your legs covered when you go blackberry picking! For a moment I pictured him shrieking like Jane when he walked into the nettle patch. I was about to point out to him that he might want to reconsider his attire, but something in his oddly attentive gaze distracted me.

Well, maybe I could work my excellent wardrobe advice into a conversation. So, I started with "Hi there. How ya doin'?"

This usually works a treat in any schoolyard situation. When he just continued fumbling in his pockets and staring at us in, what I now noticed, was an unblinking and unfriendly kind of way, I decided that I needed to learn whatever the grown-up equivalent of 'Hi there' was.

At any rate, he had a totally unique ice-breaker of his own.

Without having spoken a word to us, he simply pulled the edges of his raincoat apart and stood there – naked (as my grandmother would say) as the day he was born. Except for the boots, I guess.

I didn't know a lot about adult male anatomy, but I had changed my baby brother's nappies a time or two. I knew the basics of what we were dealing with but there was something alien and frightening about the size and insistence of it. I didn't know what it was for but I knew that this was horribly wrong.

The children all screamed, baskets and bags were dropped. Our visitor took a menacing step forward.

Any doubts I had were dissolved in that instant. I spread my arms out and stood in front of the children.

"GET AWAY FROM US!"

I had never shouted so loud before. I had hoped I could summon enough power through my voice to knock him off his bandy, hairy legs.

He stayed on his booted feet but seemed to sway a little. And he blinked.

As if on cue, the rest of the gang started screaming at a higher decibel and clung together behind me.

"YOU GO AWAY FROM US, NOW!"

The combined momentum of my shouting and their screaming seemed to push him to his tipping point.

He pulled the edges of his coat together and backed up. As we continued screaming, he continued shuffling backwards until he finally turned himself around and fell into a stumbling run across the lumpy surface of the field. He disappeared around a hedge.

Small hands grabbed me around my waist and I felt Jane trembling with sobs. The older girls looked pale and confused. Derek turned to me and said, "What was that?" I didn't know what to say.

I never did tell my parents. I don't know why, but it just seemed like such a personal event and since the fella had run off, it didn't seem like there was anything left to do.

But Peggy, Jane and Derek had told their parents and the next thing I knew, mine had me seated at the kitchen table, looking at me with a worrying sort of anxiousness.

My parents asked me if it was true about me chasing off a fella in a raincoat. I gave them what details I could, and Da nodded and looked at my mother.

"I believe that is Mr O'Hara's nephew."

She gasped a little bit and put her hand to her mouth. Shocking to hear that such things can be done by people you know, I suppose.

Da looked back at me.

"He's a bit simple. I'm afraid they have let him run about, thinking he was harmless."

"Well, he didn't harm anyone. Not really."

I don't know how I ended up defending the poor boy but, I admit, I did not do it whole-heartedly. I was years away from understanding what had happened that day, but somehow I knew that some invisible border had been crossed, some razor-thin line between innocence and its loss had been bridged. And I would, forever, have to be dragged across that bridge kicking and screaming.

The war years – and the years just after – were tough, and we weren't even fighting in the bloody thing. I was always puzzled about that, and the more the grown-ups tried to explain to me why we had rationing and shortages and hardships, the more I thought it was a load of rubbish.

For the most part, we did what we always did – we made do and carried on. My da was a builder and hauled gravel for making roads, so he always had work. We were very lucky compared to most folks. But the war was creating problems for him in a roundabout way. His business depended on trucks, and his trucks were undergoing a lot of wear and tear. New parts for cars and trucks were rare, expensive and controlled by the government. Due to 'war' measures, public vehicles had first priority for repair and maintenance. At the rate things were going, if one of Da's trucks broke down, he might have to wait till the war was over to get a replacement part.

Among builders, truck drivers, garage owners and mechanics this was a highly unsatisfactory situation. Fortunately, my da and my uncle were friends with some of the fellas who worked for the government at the parts depot.

We Irish are a very clannish lot, it's true. We look out for each other, and whatever our differences may be, we tend to all agree on one very fundamental premise – we don't like the government telling us what we can or can't do. Even if it's good for us. Right or wrong, it just isn't to be tolerated that the government should interfere in some way with our right to gainful pursuits. So, even the fellas who worked at the government depot, who knew that the imported truck parts were earmarked for public vehicles, were sympathetic to my da's plight and, in fact, they offered more than sympathy.

As I said, times were tough and, even for men who had steady jobs with the government, it was difficult to stretch a shilling when what you needed was a pound. It seemed that having access to the truck parts could be a win-win situation for all concerned: Da could keep his trucks running and the depot men could make a few extra bob. And it was only one truck part, so what was the harm?

It was agreed, therefore, that the carburettor that Da needed would be 'made available'.

In exchange for a few pounds, Da would be able to 'drop by' the depot and collect the part off the shelf – it would be helpfully marked with some twine tied around it.

The only catch was that the part would have to be collected after the depot was closed, preferably when it was getting dark. Someone was going to have to be lowered over the brick wall, make their way into the depot building and collect the part, then place it in a bag which would be raised over the wall, after which, the rope would be thrown back over to haul the parts collector to the other side.

Note two things about this plan – it would have to be a small person to do the collecting, as hauling a grown man back and forth over the wall would be difficult and noisy. And, secondly, the part would go back over the wall first, leaving the collector sitting on the wrong side of both the barrier and the law. I think you can see where this is going.

Looking back, this may have been a lot to ask of a twelve-year-old girl but I thought it was brilliant and sounded like great fun.

The night of the Great Heist was cold but clear. My da, my uncle and I arrived outside the walls of the depot, having had to park our own car a good distance away.

We kept to the shadows and crept along until we got to the part of the wall we had been told had the best access. There were some broken bricks and boards lying nearby and we used those to construct a very wobbly scaffold to help get us up to the top. Once there, the rope was tied around my waist and my da and uncle leaned across the top, keeping as low as they could, and lowered me down. It was about ten feet from the top of the wall to the ground. I had a sack in my hand and, once I touched the ground, I gave the rope a tug, I then untied it from my waist and left it hanging.

I had been given detailed instructions as to where I was to go to collect the part but, in the dark and with all the piles of parts and bits of trucks and motors all over the place – not to mention a confusing array of buildings – I got a bit disoriented. I got to one building and tried the door but it was locked up very tight. I wanted to try and kick it but knew I couldn't risk making any noise. There was supposed to be a night-watchman somewhere about, though we had been assured that all he did was sit in his hut and drink tea and read racing forms.

I poked around the building a bit and noticed a small sign that said something about buses. That's when I realised that I wasn't at the right place. I retraced my steps and, in the pitch black, headed for the outline of a building to my left. I tripped over something metal and nearly went face first into a pile of spark plugs, but managed to recover my balance at the last moment and continued down the path.

I could make out the shape of a door ahead of me, tried the handle and it opened. It squealed on its hinges like a stuck pig and I nearly fell over in a faint. Surely the night-watchman would hear that – it had seemed to echo over the entire yard. I stood still, holding my breath, the thrum of my heart filling my ears. I finally exhaled, the cloud of frosty breath steaming out and away from me.

Everything remained quiet.

It seemed safe to go ahead and peer behind the door, though I decided it was too noisy to open it any further. I slithered into the narrow opening and pulled the torch out of my pocket. I kept it pointed low as I had been told not to shine it anywhere near a window. Treading as cat-like as I could in my clunky black boots, I peered ahead of me. I was looking for the third row of shelves from the left. Halfway down would be my carburettor, neat and pretty and tied up in twine.

I found the third row and started down it, shining the torch along the surface of the second tier of shelves. Further and further I went, every step that took me away from the door seemed like a mile. Finally, I saw it – some limp, oily twine tied into a sad bow on a small, but surprisingly heavy, metal object. I plopped it into the sack and headed back, turning off the torch well before I got to the door.

Once outside, it was easy to find my way back to the wall. The rope was hanging there, completely still. I gave it a small tug and waited. A moment later it waggled to let me know that Da and Uncle Barry were ready. I tied the bag to the rope and tugged it again. It went up the wall very quickly and quietly.

I heard muffled sounds from the other side of the wall. Then, suddenly, I heard whistling and very loud footsteps and saw some lights bobbing around. That didn't seem right, so I crept right up to the wall and placed myself flat against it, facing out into the yard. I could hear some voices on the other side and then nothing.

The nothing went on for a while. A good long while, it seemed like.

I slunk into a crouch, keeping close to the wall. My back started to get cold, right through my coat, the icy bricks sucking the heat out of my skinny little body. I knew that Da and Uncle Barry should have thrown the rope over long before now but, if things had gone wrong, there was nothing for me to do but wait. I didn't own a watch so I could only look at the sky and try to judge if the stars had moved. I had no idea that it was an hour and a half before I heard a scuffling sound and a loud whisper.

"Richeen! Are ya there?"

It was my da. I called back to him in the loudest whisper I could manage.

"Yeah, I'm here!"

The rope came snaking over the wall and I grabbed it with numbed fingers. My poor hands were so stiff I had a time of it trying to tie the rope around my waist. Finally, it was done and I saw their capped heads poking over the wall as they hauled me back up. Once at the top of the wall, my da grabbed me and handed me down to Barry. They bundled me up and dashed off to where the car was parked – not where I remembered us leaving it. Once in the car, swathed in a blanket, I asked what had happened.

"Some gobshites came around, asking questions." My uncle was not at all happy. "We had to scarper."

I looked at my da.

"You left me there all by myself! I could have been caught."

Da shifted into third gear and turned and grinned at me.

"Not you. I knew you would be fine. If there is anybody in this world that would be fine doing such a thing, I knew it was my Richeen."

He gave me a wink. I grinned back at him and snuggled into the blanket, almost sorry to be heading back home so soon.

⁂

One day, I brought Mary home with me after school so that she could stay for dinner.

She stayed for three weeks.

Mary was always a quiet type, yet one of those who you could tell had a lot going on behind her steady expression. She didn't say much, but had a lot of imagination and loved to read and listen to the radio. Depth is what she had. People would always say that Mary was an example of still waters that ran deep. We all knew that things weren't great for her at home.

Her father was a labourer and was out of work more than he was in it. And her mam was a good Catholic wife, meaning she was whelping a new brother or sister for Mary just about every year. Number eight had been born just before school started.

I knew Mary was glad to get back to school. Just one more

thing that set her apart – actually liking school.

Over the summer, something about her had changed. She seemed to be living more rough than usual, her clothes a bit more unkempt, the occasional scrape or bruise. Fights with her sisters, she said.

Mind you, I had more bruises and scrapes than anyone I knew, including the boys. In my mind, they were badges of honour, a source of real bragging rights.

I had a scar on my left knee that I was extremely proud of, where I had fallen on a piece of timber that had a nail in it. I remember when I stood up and the nail was still sticking into my leg, a trickle of blood winding down my shin. Katie Feeney had screamed. It was an absolute high-point of my summer.

But for Mary, it was different.

Some days, she just walked a bit gingerly, as if her back hurt. One time, when we were picking blackberries, her sleeve got pushed up and I saw a raw, red mark that completely encircled her arm, just above her wrist.

She caught me looking at it. Her expression never changed, she just pulled her sleeve back down. I took the hint and didn't ask about it.

A couple of weeks after we had gone back to school, she had a smudge under her eye that she tried to cover with her hair. And I noticed that, for the third day in a row, she had not brought her lunch.

As we sat in a circle, in the corner of the gym, the lunchtime noise of a hundred kids burbling around us, I handed her half of my ham sandwich.

I was not unaware that there were many people who had less

than my family did. My mother went to great lengths to point it out to myself and my brother and my sisters, and frequently. It was something I just grew up knowing about. Though the scope of it escaped me, I knew that many of the families around us struggled. It is hard to explain to people now how easily we adapted to poverty back then. It was an element of nature – an inevitability, like rain. None of us had a lot, but many were teetering on a desperate edge.

Unbeknownst to us, Mary's family had teetered over that edge and fallen into desperation.

She bit into her half of the sandwich with tiny bites. She was trying to make it last, stretching out the memories of each mouthful since later it might be only the memories she would have to chew on.

Before she could finish nibbling the poor thing into molecules, I handed her my apple. She raised her eyebrows.

"I have two apples today." Which was a lie.

Mary bit into the apple and nodded.

She knew I was lying. And she knew why. She didn't make a fuss, she just ate the apple and let it go. It's good to have friends like that.

After school, she came to my house and we did the usual mucking about with the gang. As the afternoon got very late, she was in no hurry to get home. My mother asked if she would like to stay for dinner and so Mary stayed. After dinner we did our homework together. Well, she did her homework. I was rollicking around on the floor playing cars with my baby brother. Mary wrote into her copybooks so neatly and deliberately. And her book satchel was in such good order. She could actually find a pencil and a ruler when she needed it. I admit, I was a bit awestruck.

As the evening progressed, I noticed that Mary looked at the kitchen clock occasionally with a look of dread. She hated seeing the time going by. I don't know how I knew that as, at the time, she told me nothing directly. But I sensed that she was dreading something. Dreaded leaving us, dreaded going back home.

On a whim, I asked my mother if Mary could stay the night and go to school with me in the morning. I had never had a friend over on a school night before. My mother frowned at me. But with Mary hovering over my shoulder, she did not want to appear ungenerous.

"Will it be alright with your mother?" She asked.

Mary nodded. She nodded fervently.

And that was it. Over the next few days, between the two of us, we kept coming up with more excuses as to why she didn't need to go home. My mother pouted a bit, and I could tell she was put out, but she was too proud to turf Mary out. It was my da who sat down with me one night, while Mary was in the loo, and asked me what was going on. I told him what little I knew, and that wasn't much.

"Let me look into it." That was all he said.

It was years later when I learned what had happened. My father knew who Mary's father was, of course. Though they did not move in the same circles, Da and my uncle and one of our neighbours all knew where Mr Farrelly went to drink.

So, one night, after Mary's da had spent money he didn't have at the pub, the three men were waiting for him. They followed him for a bit and then cornered him in a secluded part of a quiet lane. My father spared me the details but, apparently, between the three of them they 'explained' to Mr Farrelly what they thought of a man who drank the food money and then beat his wife and children. A few cracked ribs, a broken nose and some loosened teeth apparently convinced him of the error of his ways. Especially when he was reminded that they would be keeping an eye on the family from now on.

Mr Farrelly's behaviour improved but, even better, after a couple of months, Mrs Farrelly finally found the strength to pack up her kids and move in with her sister. Mary's father was out of her life for good.

Every once in a while, over the next couple of years, I would have Mary over for dinner after school. She would always go straight home after.

⁂

It seemed like everyone in the neighbourhood helped at the Holy Ghost Fathers' farm. My grandfather worked there several mornings a week and all of us children helped over the summer.

There was certainly loads to do. At one time, the priests and brothers had been completely self-sufficient – they grew wheat, they raised dairy and beef cattle, they had poultry, pigs, ducks and sheep and there were also large vegetable and herb gardens. Now, most of the brothers had become more interested in teaching, while the priests were mostly occupied with fundraising for the church, so it was left to the parishioners to contribute to the farm work. When my granddad would go, I loved to tag along.

Dominic and Brian were there a lot. Sometimes it was because their parents were there, often it was because they had been assigned farm chores as either a penance or a punishment for some transgression at school. Hard work in the open air was supposed to cleanse them. Mostly it just cleansed them of whatever common sense they might have had.

To be fair, the farm was a paradise of play for a kid. The big stacks of hay, the huge barns full of nooks and crannies, the wide-open fields, the small sheds crammed with all kinds of weird and interesting objects. We had a fantastic time building forts and castles from hay bales, climbing up ladders, sliding down ropes. It was hard to concentrate on things like chores.

One afternoon I was playing in the piles of hay on the farm while Granddad was helping separate the ewes from the rams. Dominic was supposed to be helping to muck out the pens where Brother Brown's prized French hens were kept. He still had his shovel in his hand, but was using it to help me rearrange the bales into a stairway so that I could climb up to the edge of the loft without having to use the ladder.

We were prying a particularly tricky one into place when Brother Brown came in.

"Dominic!" He roared.

Dominic turned towards him and dropped his shovel.

"I have been looking everywhere for you!" Brother Brown looked slightly unhinged at the best of times. In his current distress, his frog-like eyes were fairly popping, and blue lines throbbed on his temples.

Dominic clumsily retrieved his shovel.

"Sorry, sir. I was just ... er, I was ... I was helping Rio."

Brother Brown snatched the shovel out of his hands.

"You are supposed to be in the hen yard!' He punctuated this with a finger that stabbed into Dominic's chest.

"You are supposed to be cleaning out the manure!" Another punctuation mark, this one nearly toppling Dominic backwards.

"Sorry, Brother Brown." Dominic put his hand on his chest, his eyes starting to water.

Brother Brown was having none of it. He grabbed Dominic by an ear and twisted.

Over Dominic's yelping, Brother Brown continued his scolding.

"Now you get into that pen and you finish your chores now! And I want to see you back here tomorrow – that's another afternoon you owe me for the aggravation you have caused me today!"

With that, he gave the ear a final twist and pushed Dominic out towards the yard, forcing the shovel into his hand as he did so.

Dominic stumbled out, one hand dragging the shovel, the other clapped over his ear. Brother Brown paid no attention to me whatsoever. He just turned on his heel and stormed out.

I don't know what made me do it. I truly don't remember having anything in particular in mind. But I picked up a clod of muck that was on the ground next to me and hurled it at Brother Brown's retreating back.

It was my bad luck to have such excellent aim. The clod of dirt exploded all over his cassock, leaving a bloom of brown debris on the pristine blackness.

He wheeled around in a way that was frighteningly fast. Years of experience being pelted by schoolboys with spit balls, I suppose. He turned to see me gawping at him like a landed guppy. His face was practically ignited with rage.

"You come here this instant, young lady!"

That seemed to me to be a very bad idea. I licked my lips and looked around for alternatives. Ah, my staircase of hay bales. That looked like a better choice.

I turned and high-tailed it up the stacks of hay and leaped up onto the lip of the overhanging hayloft. I didn't turn to look – I could hear the footsteps behind me. Brother Brown was making a beeline for my ears.

Once in the loft, I zigzagged around barrels, bags and more bales and headed for the exit. Not the ladder, mind you. Brother Brown would only follow me down and eventually his superior size would win the day (at the expense of my ears).

There was another way out – and one in which my size would be an advantage – the hay chute. This led directly down into the pens below, where the cows would normally be placidly chewing their cuds in colder weather. Today, there would be nothing there but a hay rack and some squishy piles of cow dung. Well, it would at least be a soft landing. I lunged for the opening, which was just wide enough for my shoulders and plummeted down, landing on my bottom in a mixture of mouldy hay and manure.

I heard a yelp above me, which was Brother Brown realising where I had gone, I then heard a thud and then … nothing. Until the yelling started.

I looked up and there were Brother Brown's feet, suspended in the air above me. They were twisting frantically and bits of hay and small clods of dirt were drifting down, dislodged by his panicked contortions. He was still yelling but the sound was muffled and I couldn't hear exactly what he was saying. I could guess though. I was no expert, but I suspected that Brother Brown was going to have to say a lot of Hail Marys after this.

Intending to keep the integrity of my ears intact – both from the cursing and from Brother Brown's grasp – I got up and headed for the farmyard. I found Dominic and Brian there, in the special pen for the black and white speckled hens, both shovelling piles of chicken shit into a wheelbarrow. Brian was occasionally flicking a bit off the end of his shovel towards Dominic's shoes. Dominic was ignoring him, keeping his eyes on the ground, and I could occasionally hear him sniffle.

Brian flicked some dung off his shovel at me as a greeting.

"Heya pigpen." Well, I guess I did look a mess.

"Hey yourself."

Brian leaned on his shovel. "Are you here to help, or what?"

"Nah, I'm just hiding out for a minute."

Brian grinned. "From who?"

"Brother Brown. He's stuck in the hay chute."

Dominic looked up for the first time.

"Stuck?"

I shrugged.

"Yeah, he followed me down and got stuck. He's gonna be in a right mood when he gets out."

The boys started laughing. Brian punched me in the shoulder.

"Boy, he will won't he?"

"Yeah." I looked at Dominic. "And he's already in a bad enough temper today."

His face clouded.

"Yeah, he is."

"Someone needs to tell him to be nicer." I wasn't sure who that would be, but it seemed like it needed to be done. "He's just a big bully."

Dominic slid his shovel under a heap of smelly white solids.

"Well, no one is gonna do that. No one cares what the brothers do to us kids."

"Someone needs to."

A head poked around the fence, a priest's collar around its neck.

"Have you children seen Brother Brown?"

A moment of respectful silence. And then, as one, we all shook our heads. The head, and the collar, disappeared. We looked at each for a moment. In the quiet, we could hear the clucking from the hens inside their neat shed, where they were enclosed while their yard was being cleaned.

"Lads," I said. "I have an idea."

Part Two

The Road More Travelled

Growing up was more fun for my sisters than for me. They liked all the dressing up, the lipstick, the nylons and high heels, the parties and dancing and, of course, boys. I liked all of that, too, but I didn't see the need for any hurry. It seemed to me we would have all the rest of our lives to be grown-ups and such a precious short time to be kids.

What a nightmare for my parents – three girls in various stages of hormonal surges. My da instituted some very strict rules to try and keep us in line – we had to be home by twelve sharp. No ifs, ands or buts, no excuses, no sob stories and all hell to pay if curfew was violated. Cinderella never faced such a dire fate when the clock struck midnight. This was meant to be an obstacle to our misbehaving. We saw it as more of a challenge. As my sisters were more interested in going out than I was, at first I was in charge of covering for them. This could take several forms – one was the Ever Open Window in my room so that they could come home by midnight, like good girls, make a show of getting ready for bed, and then sneak out of my bedroom window and go back out for more. The window was left unlocked so that they could also climb back into it in the wee hours of the morning. Then they had to be very quiet about making their way down the hall to their own rooms.

Occasionally, either Mam or Da tried to catch us out and would do a surprise inspection of our rooms. After being found out that way once, we learned to stuff some clothes under the covers and place scarves wrapped around hair curlers, or even bits of old wigs on the pillows. Fortunately, once they saw what they wanted to see they never thought to turn on the light or we would have been in dire trouble.

Eventually, after I finished school, I started to get interested in going out, too. I had trained to be a window dresser and found that I enjoyed my new incarnation as an independent girl with an income. So, with a few bob in my pocket and a growing circle of friends, the night life started to have its appeal. And for us, the night life meant music.

I can't remember ever not singing. My Granny Murphy had been a singer, all of my uncles sang songs, starting with nursery rhymes when I was little and then, later, the ballads. After a Sunday dinner or a Saturday card game, it wasn't at all unusual for everyone to sit around the kitchen and sing songs, recite poetry or tell stories. So, when my friends and I would go out of an evening and we ended up sitting in a pub and someone would have a guitar – well, I always managed to have a song to sing.

We all did.

There was a gang of us that became regulars at some of the best haunts – such as O'Donoghues and The Wren's Nest – and a few were serious musicians. Singers and players such as Luke Kelly and Ronnie Drew were in the mix, well before their days of playing together in the legendary band, The Dubliners. Besides the pubs and the get-togethers, there were also road trips. We would load up into some of the old bangers that we called cars and head out to places in the country. Sometimes there was a fleadh or a festival going on, sometimes we just knew of a great pub that would let us play, give us some sandwiches, and then let us sleep on the kitchen floor. The weekends often turned out to be closer to a week which created problems for those of us who were meant to get back to our jobs on a Monday morning!

I remember one weekend in particular, when the Clancy Brothers were playing in a town out in the country. We had all headed up there only to find the place packed and hardly any room for us. But then who did I see stuck outside with the rest of us but the great fiddler, Ted Furey.

I called to the fella inside at the door that Ted Furey wanted to come in with his fiddle, and that worked like magic. The door was opened and we all got to worm our way into the crowded session, and I got to sit next to Ted while he played. Ted was in his seventies at the time and, besides being a wonderful musician, he was a great storyteller. He also, famously, set an example that many up-and-coming Irish musicians would imitate for years afterwards – he had a glorious beard. As the evening progressed, the music got more exhilarating, the drink was flowing and Ted's bow arm was flying around like a mad thing. I was in the flow of it myself and enjoying every minute, so it was very jarring when the fiddle music next to me suddenly stopped with a screech.

I turned to look and saw a very perplexed Ted with his hand clenched around the neck of his fiddle. He looked at me, not moving his head, just turning his eyes.

"What's the matter, Ted?"

He waggled the neck of the fiddle a bit. The fiddle did not move away from his neck. I looked closer and saw why.

His beard had gotten tangled into the fiddle strings!

I took a good look and did my best to get him loose. What a mess, I'd never seen the likes of it before and haven't seen it since. Those whiskers were tied tight in there as if little hands had made a thousand tiny knots. I finally had to tell him. "Ted, we're going to have to cut you out." His eyes widened with alarm, but he didn't say no.

I started digging through my handbag for my small pair of manicure scissors. Yes, I carry scissors, and a screwdriver and a few other things, too.

He nodded and I leaned over to start the delicate operation. Several curious people were now looking on.

"Just one thing."

I looked up at him, trying not to tug on his chin.

"Yes?"

"Do whatever you need ta for the beard – but don't cut the strings!"

Now, that was a real musician.

In the midst of all this fun, I became good friends with a girl my own age named Doris, who was a great singer and a load of laughs. Even more importantly, she was one of the ones who had a car, so she was a vital part of the group. Besides the pubs and the singing, she was also an avid dancer. At the time, the favourite dance hall on the southside of the city was the Olympic. Now, don't think I spent all of my younger years with skinned knees, running wild, I also learned all the things girls needed to know – including dancing. And I was darn good at it, as well. So, it became a thing for Doris and me on Saturday nights to get on our nylons and lipstick and head to the dance. Doris had a fair-haired, light kind of beauty and an easy smile – the boys flocked around her. I was more of the dark haired, well-cushioned sort, but I was never afraid to talk to anyone, could enjoy a pint or two without getting stupid and could dance all night. So, in our own ways, we each had our appeal.

One of my first conquests was a good-looking young fella named Tommy Ferguson. He was nineteen, tall and slender with brown, wavy hair and a dimple when he smiled. Light on his feet, he was one of the best dancers there. The other great dancer was his identical twin brother.

Yes, Tommy and Timmy, the Ferguson twins. What a pair. It was like two scoops of your favourite ice-cream in one cone, and I was never one to say no to dessert.

Tommy was the first one to ask me out. We went to see a film one Friday evening, then we went for a coffee. I was home by twelve … and then out the window and off we went to go dancing till *very* late.

I liked Tommy a lot, he was great fun and not at all bad to look at, but I wasn't interested in settling down with something like a boyfriend. Not *one* boyfriend, anyway.

So, one Saturday at the Olympic, Tommy wasn't there but Timmy was and, wouldn't you know it, he asked me out for the following Thursday! Lovely.

So, we went to a film and then out for a coffee. I was home for my curfew … then, whoosh, out the window again and we were off to a ceili somewhere. Well, they were twins, so perhaps it's not surprising that the dates were similar.

I have to say, I had a lovely time with each of them. Doris asked me which one I liked better, which seemed to mean that I was supposed to choose one. That seemed highly unfair to me – I liked them both, why not have both?

And, so, I started a juggling act that Barnum and Bailey would have envied.

Tommy might call and ask me to go out on Wednesday, and then Timmy might call and ask me out for a Thursday. I would generally try to find out where the other one was going to be on a given night so that I could make sure that my date and I were on the other side of town.

Sometimes my plans got so convoluted that I could hardly keep them straight – was it Tuesday with Timmy or Thursday with Tommy? Finally, one week, I decided to get back out on the playing field and spend my Saturday night with Doris and the gang at the Olympic. Tommy had phoned and asked me to go to a film – I told him I had to babysit. So, he said he would go and play cards with his mates. Timmy had phoned and wanted to go and listen to some music somewhere – I told him I was coming down with a cold, so, he said he would go along on his own and meet up with some of his friends there.

With the coast clear, I slapped on some lippy and met up with Doris at the dance hall. Things were busy and the music was great – I had just finished a fabulous spin around the dance floor with a nice fella from Crumlin, when I felt a tap on my shoulder.

I turned around and was gobsmacked to see Tommy – or maybe Timmy – standing there.

"Hiya darling," he was grinning. Tommy, I was pretty sure.

"Didn't have to babysit after all? You shoulda phoned me!"

Oops. "It was very last minute," I said. I looked over Tommy's shoulder to see the fella from Crumlin give me an odd look and then walk away and start talking to another girl. Damn it.

I looked desperately around for Doris to see if I could give her the signal that meant 'Bail me out'. No sign of her.

Tommy put his hands on my waist.

"Well, since we're both here now let's get out there and have some fun."

"Er … yeah, well, just a minute. Need to catch my breath." I was scanning the crowd for Doris desperately now.

Then I felt a tap on my shoulder. At last! Reprieve! I turned around with a big smile on my face, expecting to see my pal. No such luck.

"What the hell is going on here?" It was Timmy – or maybe Tommy? The other one, at any rate.

Now it was Tommy's turn. "What does it look like? Me and Rio are about to dance."

"Yeah?" Timmy (or Tommy? I was getting confused now) grabbed my arm. "I thought you had a cold and couldn't go out tonight? Why would you be too sick to go out with me but well enough to go out dancing?"

Tommy (maybe?) pulled on my other arm. "What are you on about? Go out with you?"

"Yeah, we were gonna go somewhere. What's it to ya?"

The conversation was getting louder and going on over my head, back and forth, as if I wasn't there. Not being there did, in fact, seem like a good idea. I tried to wriggle free. Timmy let go, Tommy held on tighter. Or vice versa.

"She was supposed to babysit tonight, otherwise she was gonna go out with me!"

"What? You're a liar!"

"No, *you're* the fucking liar."

It was getting messy. Though, interestingly, in the light of brotherly competition, neither one of them seemed to have considered the lying that I had obviously been doing. Thank goodness.

I wriggled my arm free and stepped out of the way. This seemed to be the signal they had been waiting for – now they could start pummelling the bejesus out of each other, free and clear. I stood still for a moment, partly in shock but also just a wee bit delighted that I had two lads fighting over me. How exciting! Some of the other fellas there jumped in and started trying to pry the pair of them apart. As I stood there, gaping, I felt yet another tap on my shoulder.

I turned and this time it *was* Doris.

"Hell's bells, you'd best get outta here."

She hauled me out to the front and we sat on the steps and waited for the noise to die down. Doris lit a cigarette and eyed me appraisingly.

"Well, aren't you the little heartbreaker?"

"Ah, shit, I never meant it to turn out like that." Guilt was starting to rear its ugly head at me. Just a bit. "I feel terrible. No more twins for me. Bloody not worth it."

Doris exhaled a long stream of smoke and watched it thoughtfully as it curled into the cold evening air.

"Oh, I don't know." She took another pull. "They're pretty cute."

She looked down at me. "And they're available again, yeah?"

"You've got to be joking."

She shrugged and smiled. No, she was definitely not joking. Cheeky bitch!

༈

I suppose I could have carried on that way forever. It was a good life – I enjoyed my job, I never had any empty time on my hands and always had just enough money to do what I wanted. Music and dancing filled up my evenings and weekends. Now, mind you, my parents would not have thought that all of that carrying on was at all appropriate for a young woman who had a job to get to every day. I couldn't go swanning out the door every night and say, "I'm off to the pub". That would not have gone down well.

So, instead, I started taking classes at the Red Cross every Thursday night: first-aid and what not. At least, that's what I told my parents. For weeks, I kept up the pretence that I was learning how to make tourniquets and give mouth-to-mouth resuscitation (well, at least that wasn't too far off the mark) when, of course, I was going out and having a few pints and singing and dancing. It seemed harmless enough.

Then, one day, I was in town shopping with my mother, weaving through the crowds on O'Connell Street. It was a lovely, bright day.

Suddenly, there was a loud screech, a horrible rasping of metal on metal, as someone's brakes tried desperately to bring a car to a stop. A sickening thump was followed by a chorus of screams and several people began calling for help. A rush of footsteps behind us made us turn to see what had happened.

Out in the street, just behind us, merely a few feet from the kerb, a crowd was gathering. I could hear some folks exclaiming and even whimpering. They were all standing in front of a car that was incongruously stopped in the middle of the busy flow of traffic.

The two of us edged a bit closer, but there was already a thin wall of people surrounding whatever had happened.

"What's going on?" My mother asked the nearest man.

"Accident," he said. "Fella got knocked down by a car."

My mother pursed her lips as if annoyed and then pushed her way through the crowd, dragging me by the elbow.

"Stand back!" She called out in her commanding voice. I was thinking to myself, what in blue blazes is she interfering for?

Then she turned to me and pulled me forward.

"Everyone out of the way – my daughter here knows first-aid!"

Oh bloody fucking hell. Someone who had been kneeling

next to the man stood up.

"Oh dear Jesus, he just stepped out in front of me – I couldn't stop." Tears were streaming down his face.

"Ah, it's alright now. You just need to keep away for the moment."

Everyone else got silent and looked at me. I could feel their fear and expectation, aimed at me like arrows. I could also feel my armpits getting damp.

I looked down.

It was a man in workman's boots and dusty dungarees, in his forties it looked like, sprawled awkwardly on the pavement. His leg had an unnatural bend to it at the knee. There was blood on the side of his face from a cut on his forehead. The blood wasn't gushing, mind you, but it was trickling along well enough. His eyes flickered a bit and he moaned a little. My stomach decided to rise up and say hello to my tonsils. I turned my head to look away, but there was my mother looking right back at me, frowning.

"Well?"

I cleared my throat, encouraging my stomach to get back down where it belonged.

"Glrrrgl." I managed to get that out anyway.

"What does that mean?" Mother was glaring a bit now.

Someone else decided to add to my misery.

"What should we do, Miss?"

I knew what I wanted to do – I wanted to get the hell out of there. My tormenter continued. "Does he need to be resuscitated?"

Oh my God, was this crowd of people expecting me to

clamp my lips onto this poor, bleeding fellow and start exchanging breath – and saliva? While they stood around and watched? What a load of sick bastards.

I looked around, searching for an exit. But no, there was my ma – watching and waiting, like an emotional piranha.

I licked my lips and decided, blood or no blood, it was time to be decisive.

"Everyone stay back!" I held my arms out as if trying to fend off a horde of invading Mongols. "No one touch him. Has anyone called an ambulance?"

Someone from the back answered, "Yeah, someone in Arnotts just rang them. They're on the way."

Thank Christ. Perhaps I would only need to wing it for a few more minutes. The man was stirring a bit more now, trying to move his arms.

I leaned towards him. "Now, now. Just lie still, don't try and move. Help is on the way."

My ma was smiling now, basking in my obvious command of the situation.

"Yes, everyone just stay back, like she says." She leaned towards me. "Very good, dear. Well done."

It wasn't too long before the ambulance arrived and they started getting the poor fella sorted. He was a bit dazed still, but otherwise seemed okay – except for that leg.

The first ambulance man on the scene had looked around and said, "Has anyone moved this man? Has he been shifted about in any way?"

Everyone in the crowd shook their heads, I made a forceful pronouncement of, "No, we didn't move him."

"Good." That was all he said, and then they got to work and took the man away.

When I announced the following week that I was no longer going to take the first-aid courses, my mother just smiled and patted me on the shoulder. She assumed that it was because I didn't need them. I was obviously already an expert.

⁊❦❧⁊

Just as my childhood had passed all too quickly, it seemed that this phase of my life was destined to be all too short as well. An insidious affliction was destroying the very fabric of my social structure. One by one, my friends were falling victim to a force that plunged their lives forever into a turmoil from which they could not escape.

They were all getting married and reproducing like rabbits.

Tommy Ferguson was one of the first – no, neither Doris nor myself landed that one. Then Peggy, then Brendan, Lola, Kitty and then Timmy. But it was when Doris announced that she was getting married that I knew that a chapter in our lives had just been closed. And there I was, without even a fucking bookmark.

Doris married a man who was a few years older than the rest of us. She had met him at one of our weekends away somewhere. His name was Damien and he had a good job, selling feed and fertiliser to farmers, so he travelled a lot. They settled into a little house in Lucan and before I knew what was what, she was pregnant – with twins.

My circle of Saturday night dance partners was getting

smaller and smaller by the week. One night at the Olympic I met someone new – a nattily dressed fella with wavy, gingery hair who had an air about him that seemed different than everyone else. He was a bit more serious, yet still liked to have fun. He had a good job as a butcher, right there in the city and he took to me straightaway. His name was Hughie Hogarty.

We took up together as dance partners and then started seeing each other during the week for films and music sessions, and what have you. He was a singer himself, so we found ourselves with a lot in common, sharing a lot of the same interests and pastimes. What can I say? One thing led to another and, the next thing I knew, I was struck down by the same affliction that had stolen away all of my friends.

Hughie had a sister, Geraldine, who was a talented seamstress so she made me a wedding dress and, at the age of twenty-two, I marched down the aisle and my father gave me away. I am not sure which of us cried more.

And that was it. In a flurry of lace and flowers, I had surrendered to the current that was carrying us all forward, away from the known shores of our younger selves and into some unexplored territory where the footing was less certain. Both the girl with the scabby knees and fearless heart and the teenager with the easy smile and cheeky humour were in some small way diminished.

Now, I was Rio Hogarty.

I may have been a city girl, but I was not ignorant about country ways. I had spent a good deal of time helping out at the Holy Ghost Fathers' farm, for one thing. But, although I knew that Hughie was a butcher, I had envisioned him as working in a tidy shop, wearing a pristine apron, standing behind the counter slicing pork chops and wrapping Sunday roasts in white paper.

For some reason we had never talked much about the details of what he did at his work on a daily basis. I did not know, for example, that he was literally a butcher – that he slaughtered animals and then cleaned them.

Well, I guess every new bride has to have her rude awakenings. Mine occurred on the first day he came home from work carrying a big lumpy bag. He brought it into the house and dropped it on the kitchen floor.

"Here you go, " he said. And then immediately walked to the kitchen sink and started scrubbing very thoroughly with hot sudsy water up to his elbows.

I looked at the sack. It was grimy and stained and had a horrible smell coming from it. I knew this was not a thoughtful gift or a romantic token. I had the sneaking suspicion that I really did not want to open it all. I peered at him over the top of my glasses.

"And ...?"

"And what? It's my work clothes. They need to be cleaned. I have another set to wear tomorrow, but those will need to be scrubbed so's I can have them for the day after."

"They need to be cleaned?"

"Yep."

I untied the string at the end of the bag and peeked in.

Holy God, it was as if someone had stuffed the insides of a slaughter-house into a linen wrapper. His shirt, apron and gloves were caked with blood and some solid bits that I did not even want to contemplate.

"Bloody hell! How is that supposed to be cleaned?"

"Well, I used to take it to the laundry over on Capel Street after work and collect it the next day. They boil it all off, I think." He dried his hands on a towel and turned to me with a smile.

"But now that I have a wife, I won't be needing to do that, will I?"

He stood there and kept smiling. I sat there and kept, well, NOT smiling. Eventually his smile started to wobble a bit. Apparently, in the dreams of certain bachelors, their newly-bound brides approach their laundry with enthusiasm. If so, this was one former bachelor who was about to have his soapy dreams shattered.

"So, you want me to deal with this, do you?"

He tried smiling again. "Yes, dear."

I grabbed the bag, stood up and marched out the kitchen door to the bin in the yard. I pulled up the lid, dropped the bag in, banged the lid down and came back into the kitchen.

He started to splutter.

"But … but … no … you can't throw them away. Jesus, I need those … they need to be clean, you can't just pitch them out."

I put my hands on my hips.

"You want them clean, you can take 'em back to the laundry. That's what a laundry is for."

He blinked at me for a minute, then went out and collected his bundle from the rubbish bin. From that day on, he took his butcher's clothes to the laundry at the end of every working day.

And from that day, the honeymoon was definitely over.

❧❦❧

I gave up the job as a window dresser shortly after I discovered that I was pregnant but sitting around, gestating, wasn't my style. Geraldine was running a dressmaking business out of her kitchen and it occurred to me that we could do better than that. So, Hughie and Geraldine and I took the lease on a shop called 'Michels' and went into business. She did the dressmaking and I did the more work-a-day end of it. Not a surprise, I suppose, that my gift for gab (some would say my gift for *endless* gab) made me excellent at sales. It didn't even seem like work to chat with people all day and convince them to purchase a communion dress for their granddaughter or a new hat for church.

I also started driving a small van for transporting supplies back and forth to Geraldine and to the shop. I quite liked that. I also found that I enjoyed the challenge of dealing with suppliers. Being an avid dancer, I found that negotiations were also dance-like – and I loved the bobbing and weaving of it, the give and take, the moving together then moving apart. Just like a fast dance, it kept me on my toes.

By the age of twenty-three, I was the mother of a baby girl, running a shop, managing a household and still going out to the sing-songs and festivals. We Irish are a resilient people. We learned how to continue to answer the call of the bards even as our lives became more complex – it just meant mastering the logistics of having small children in tow. Though some of the sparkling conversation included rather a lot of debate about the best ways to deal with nappy rash and there were more frequent breaks for bottles of milk and nap time than for a round of pints, we carried on almost where we had left off.

Doris had her hands full with the twin boys. Her husband was away a lot, so she would sometimes help me at the shop – drive the van or stock shelves – and we got into a routine of going to the Dandelion Market, on Dublin's southside, on Saturday and Sunday mornings. The square would be a hodge-podge of stalls and tables, with some folks selling things from the boot of their car or the back of their van or truck, with everything you could think of (and many you wouldn't have even dreamt of) on offer. We loved prowling through the stacks and boxes, hunting for the best bargains on household items like laundry soap and toilet paper. We got to know the traders and the other regular customers well, and enjoyed the company and the banter as much as the shopping.

Even though her husband had a good job, Doris always seemed to be struggling for cash. I knew she had more expenses than me, what with her having two children while I only had the one, but it still seemed as if Damien was leaving her short of her housekeeping money every week. His business trips on the road seemed to be keeping him away longer and longer. Fortunately, she had her mother nearby to help her with the boys, but, even so, the strain of it was getting to her, I could tell.

Then, one day, Damien went off to work and never came back.

There was no word from him. Days went by, and Doris

waited. Then it was a week. The week turned into several weeks. She phoned him at work and would get fobbed off by various people saying he was out on the road and couldn't get in touch with her, telling her not to worry, that they were sure he was fine.

But there was no money coming in.

On a morning about six weeks after Damien had disappeared, I was behind the counter at Michels, when the shop door flew open and Doris burst in, a newspaper in her hand.

That stupid, arse-licking, bloody fucker! She shouted, waving the newspaper and then throwing it onto the counter in front of me.

Thank goodness there were no customers in the shop at the time. I saw the curtain to the back room twitch a little and Geraldine peeked out, looking completely terrified. She saw it was Doris, realised it was probably perfectly logical to be terrified, and let the curtain fall back.

"Jesus, Doris, what's this all about? You look like you could eat the face off someone."

She slapped her hand on the newspaper.

Look at it! Page seven. Just bloody fuckin' look at it. She folded her arms and started pacing around the shop.

I adjusted my glasses and opened the paper. She had thoughtfully folded it so that page seven was on top. The social page. There was a nice picture of the stone church near Stephen's Green with a sharply dressed family coming down the steps, the husband shaking hands with the priest as they left the Sunday service. There was a wife and two small children, a boy and a girl. I noted that neither the wife's hat nor the girl's dress had come from my shop. Hmph!

I looked quickly at the rest of the page and didn't see anything that looked like it would be of particular interest to Doris.

"See?" She jabbed her finger on the page, nearly impaling it.

"Do you see what that slimy shit has been up ta?"

"Doris, I don't have a clue what you're on about."

Jesus, look at the picture! Don't you see who that is? It's fucking Damien!

"Wha'?" I looked again. Bloody hell, it did look like him, now that I knew what I was looking for. I looked at the caption beneath the photo. "Mr and Mrs Damien Flannery, with their children Margaret and Robert, leaving Sunday mass…"

I couldn't stop staring at it.

"Do ya see?" Doris stabbed at it again. "Mister and bloody *Missus* Flannery – and THEIR children! Bloody hell, what about OUR children?"

"My God, he must have been married for years."

"I know!" She finally stopped her agitated pacing and slumped down onto the edge of a nearby shelf. "All this time when I thought he was on the road, he was really with *them*."

"Christ." I looked at her. "So now what? Can we get him arrested?"

Her lip started to tremble. "I don't know. Would that help? Then there'd be two families with the daddy in jail." She shrugged. "I don't know what to do."

We both just stared at the newspaper page for a while. I didn't know what to tell her, the whole thing seemed insane.

In the end, there was nothing for it but for Doris to carry on with her life and raise the twins on her own. Damien never contacted them again – and he never sent her so much as a sixpence.

So, now cash became a critical problem for her and the two little lads. I didn't have enough work for her at the shop to be of much help. As careful as she tried to be with her money, and even with some help from her family, I knew Doris was having a hard time of it.

One Saturday, we were at the Dandelion Market as usual: The bargains were a necessity now, not a lark. I was surprised to see one of my old friends there – not shopping, but standing near the back of a van, selling some canned goods out of a stack of boxes. It was Annie, Jane's older sister.

I trotted over to chat with her and dragged Doris along. I knew Annie had been married a good while back and had a son who had some health problems. While Doris poked around, I chatted with Annie. I was expecting to see her husband around somewhere, but no – like Doris, Annie had been left on her own, with a handicapped son to raise.

When I asked her how she was getting on, she explained to me that she and Jane would drive the van around, collecting bits and bobs from manufacturers and discount retail stores that were getting rid of damaged or cast-off goods. They would get them for a song and then sell them for a very decent profit at the Dandelion Market or other markets in and around Dublin.

The term 'profit' caught Doris's ear.

"What kinda profits are we talking about?"

Annie looked about and then leaned over and whispered to

us how much money she was clearing for herself every week.

"Bloody blue balls!" Doris was goggle-eyed.

"Well done." I gave Annie a pat on the arm. "That's a living wage, alright."

Annie was all smiles, but soon got busy with other customers and Doris and I moved on.

"Jesus, Rio, there's a fierce amount of money to be made in this street tradin'. Who'd a thought?"

"Sure enough. It'd be a lot of work, driving around collecting all the stuff from the wholesalers, mind you."

Doris stopped and grabbed my elbow.

"Yeah, and here I am with time on my hands."

"Yeah, so?"

"*You* have a van."

I grinned. "Bloody blue balls! I think we're about to go into the street tradin' business!"

᠅᠅

Seven adults, five children, three musical instruments and two vans – we were off on one of our usual summer holidays.

Doris, Hughie and I took turns driving. Our plan was to have no plan, and that always seemed to work out for the best. We took off on a Friday afternoon and headed west, towards the sea. We had Tom the Fiddler with us, and Olive the singer, and Rusty the concertina player, and Billy the guitarist, and so we always found a pub to stop in and do some singing and playing. We all took turns keeping the kids entertained.

We had stopped in the dark, along the side of the road on

Friday evening, having found what looked like a particularly nice and quiet place to park the vans and get everyone settled into their sleeping bags on the grassy earth. In the dark, we could tell that we had a nice stone wall to separate us from the road, so it seemed a perfect setting. It was very quiet and peaceful all night. And with good reason.

We awoke in the morning to discover, in the revealing light of day, that we had, in fact, spent the night in a small graveyard! We packed the kids up and whisked them out of there before they could cop on. It gave me the shivers, at any rate.

West and west we continued, finally landing on a beach late the following day, at Ballybunion in County Kerry. The kids splashed in the cold water and we made a small campfire where we toasted some sandwiches and huddled under blankets and told each other stories and sang songs until we all fell asleep. It had been a gorgeous evening but, during the night, some of us were infested with sand fleas.

The next day was bright but a bit windy and we were sitting along the edge of the road that ran by the seaside, the kids playing on a sandy bank, while Doris and I picked the fleas out of Tom the Fiddler's hair. We had been on the road for three days now, and I think it was starting to show. Before too long we heard the clip-clop of a horse's hooves and the kids jumped up and down in excitement.

"Look, look, it's a horse!"

Coming down the road, at a leisurely pace, was a stunning silvery grey horse with a white mane. Astride it, looking for all the world as if he belonged in a saddle, was a bearded man who was looking at us with a huge grin.

He looked familiar, but why would I know anyone riding a horse down a road in Ballybunion?

He was still smiling, so I smiled back. The closer he got, the more familiar he looked.

Jesus, it was Ronnie Drew!

He pulled the horse up next to us and the kids immediately swarmed around. He looked down, his eyes crinkling at the sight of us swaddled in blankets, picking at poor Tom's flea-infested head.

"Rio, is that you? Jesus, yas look like a bunch of beggars!"

Which absolutely delighted the children. The thought of being a roving band of beggars sounded like a grand adventure to them, no doubt.

"So, what about yourself?" I asked. "Are you playing music in town?"

"Not at all. Strictly on holidays." He patted the horse's neck. He really did seem a natural up there.

"I didn't know you knew anythin' about horses, Ronnie." That was Doris, who was giving up on the hunt for fleas. Tom continued scratching at his scalp.

"Oh, I love them. Always have – get myself a holiday where I can be with horses any time I can. How about you lot? Singin' and playin', are ya?"

"That's the plan. We'll be heading into the pub later and get ourselves a meal and see if we can get a session going."

"Ah, you'll have a great time. Lovely people down there."

We chatted a bit more and then he trotted that gorgeous horse down the lane and we didn't see him the rest of our weekend. That evening, we popped into the local and had our first decent hot meal in days. I remember ordering each of us a dinner, but it seemed that the landlady kept bringing heaped plates of food that just kept coming out of nowhere. There were so many of us, it was hard to keep track and I began to think I was imagining things. At the end of the night, I braced myself for a huge bill but, when I tried to pay, the landlady shook her head.

"Oh no, you're all sorted," she said. "Your friend Ronnie was in here earlier and said to feed the whole lot of yas whatever you wanted. He's taken care of it."

I was stunned. He had paid ahead of time for huge dinners for all twelve of us. He was such an unassuming, quietly generous man.

It was many months later that I bumped into Ronnie again at a session in Dublin. I managed to get him alone for two minutes and tell him how much I appreciated the lovely dinner he had made possible for the whole gang of us.

He just laughed. "Well, you looked like such a bunch of starvin' beggars, it was the least I could do." Then he winked at me and said something I'll never forget.

"You know, Rio," he said, "you're the only one who ever says thank you."

❧❦❧

Another weekend, another cavalcade of cars – myself, Doris, Hughie, all of the kids, Luke Kelly, Olive, Tom the Fiddler and … well, a whole lot of us. We had set out a bit later than usual, with no better plan than to head to the sea.

I was the lead driver and, as we got to County Clare, I kept heading west because I knew that was where the sea was. There were two problems, though: it was getting dark, and the roads were very winding. I would start out on a road that seemed to be going west and then it would twist itself around and we would end up heading God-knows where.

Every time we would make a turn, I would expect to see the glimmer of water somewhere ahead of me, but no such luck. Just more trees. And hedgerows. And sheep. Lots of sheep.

Eventually, even the most forbearing carload of children and musicians can get surly. It was time to find somewhere to stretch our legs, have a pee and a pint, and figure out where we were. Unfortunately, there didn't seem to be anything but farms anywhere around for miles.

After one more hollered, "Where are we?" I announced that we would stop at the very next pub we came to, even if it wasn't anywhere near the sea.

That shut everyone up for a bit and made the whole lot of them peer very intensely for any possible pubs.

"There're some lights there! It looks like a town!"

Hallelujah.

"Alright, everyone," I announced, "we're heading there." Though I hadn't a clue where we were.

The town was very small but the high street was called Fisherstreet, so I felt a bit smug about bringing us at least close to the sea. It was not difficult to locate the first pub – a cozy-looking place called O'Connors. We all traipsed in like a horde of invading barbarians, brash and loud-mouthed.

And then we stopped in our tracks.

It looked like something out of a picture postcard. The cozy room and a small crackling fire, with three fellas who looked like they had just finished doing some very difficult work involving either sheep or hay wagons sitting there, intent on their music, making sounds that lifted the heart and the spirit like a misty miracle. Whistle and flute and concertina – oh, what music. We were transfixed.

Luke looked at me and I looked at him. We walked towards the music and the whole crowd of us settled ourselves near the fire to listen. The three of them paid us no mind. The other folks in the room glanced at us and then continued to chat amongst themselves in Irish. They would look at us, mutter, perhaps followed by some slightly snide sniggering.

I finally decided we couldn't have this 'us' versus 'them' mentality going on all night. If some ice needed to be broken, I was going to be the Titanic. If we sank, I'd take them all with me. So, I piped up rather loudly to one of my friends with, "I guess they think we don't understand what they're saying."

Followed by silence.

Then one of the locals said, "Oh, so ya speak Irish do ya?"

I turned and gave him a big smile.

"No, but I always know when I'm being talked about!"

That got a laugh from both sides and the iceberg was definitely deflected. We listened to the music, clapped and danced, and then eventually we all joined in, our instruments blending with the three lads'. They turned out to be three locals who were brothers – Micho, Gussie, and Pakie – the Russells.

We had intended to just stop and get fuelled up, ask for directions and then head on to the sea, but the music was so good, the food and drink so plentiful and the hospitality so generous, that we just didn't feel like leaving. A lady up the road who had a Bed and Breakfast let us all sleep on her kitchen floor after we told her we couldn't afford rooms. Over the next few days, we got a lot of our sandwiches and drinks for free in return for playing music. People from the area kept coming in and the music would just get better and better – Sunday rolled around and none of us wanted to leave.

I remember several phone calls made on Monday morning to Dublin from some of us who had to make excuses as to why we weren't coming to work. If all the employers had put their heads together they might have been alarmed at the sudden outbreak of some mysterious 'flu'. Monday came and went. Then Tuesday. By Wednesday, there were a few in our party who would have no jobs to go back to. Ah, but that seemed a fair price to pay at the time.

Every night was full of fun and talk, stories and music – and dancing. We felt like we had landed in heaven. It turned out that my directional instincts weren't too far off – we were at the seashore. Only instead of reaching the more touristy Lisdoonvarna, we had landed in the unknown quantity of Doolin. I had never even seen the place on a map. It occurred to me, more than once, that I couldn't recall exactly how we had got there.

During the day we had loads of things to do as well. We had gorgeous scenery to walk through, sheep that the children were sure wanted to be chased, and we could go to the shore and let the kids splash around. And there, on the horizon, floating like pieces of a god's broken dream, were the Aran Islands. Inis Mór,

Inis Meáin and Inis Oírr. As soon as I saw them, I knew I wanted to go.

The easy way, of course, would have been to take the ferry, but that was also the most expensive way. Fortunately, I had connections.

One evening a big fella with a personality too large to be contained in such a small pub, had rolled into the session. He knew everyone there and had been telling them some uproarious stories in Irish. When he noticed us interlopers, he deigned to grace us with his stories in English and it wasn't too long before we were told that we were in the presence of Rory, the self-proclaimed King of Inis Oírr.

According to him, his was a small but mighty kingdom. Mostly 'peopled' by sheep and donkeys. And lonely, apparently, as he was the only one who recognised his divine right to rule. He made his living as a farmer and fisherman and I was immediately drawn to his larger-than-life personality and his infectious humour. But, even more importantly, he had a nice currach.

For those of you who don't know, or who have the sort of mind that might have put a salacious connotation on that, I will explain that a currach is a type of boat. Sorry to disappoint some of you. It's a traditional Irish boat of the islands, small and canoe-like, made of hides stretched over a wooden frame. Well, I don't think Rory was that staunch a traditionalist. No one really used hides any more, a waterproof canvas was more the norm in modern-day Ireland. But it is still a very different thing from the usual boat – no solid planking under your feet, for a start. Rory would sail or paddle, depending on the weather, his currach from the island to Doolin and back, and I thought that sounded marvellous. I convinced him to take myself and Doris over one afternoon.

The weather was dry but the sky was frowning with puckered clouds that were biding their time until it would be most inconvenient for the rainfall. The sea was, according to Rory, only mildly choppy. Good God. I was trying to imagine what 'very' choppy was like.

We had to take our shoes off, wade into the water a bit, and then climb in. The breeze was strong but not gusty, and Rory had the sail up. He shoved us away from the shore and we headed to the island.

Rory nattered the whole time, full of stories of fish and whales and seabirds and shipwrecks. It made the time fly. At one point, a particularly aggressive wave knocked us a bit sideways and Doris and I lurched dangerously close to the edge of the boat.

"Watch out there! Hold on tight!" the king commanded.

"No worries," I said, "I can swim."

Rory snorted.

"Bloody useless that."

"Swimming? I would think it's about the best thing someone in a currach could know."

He snorted again. Regally, I'm sure.

"No man who travels in a currach would waste his time learning to swim."

I thought he was being deliberately difficult but if he was trying to bait me to ask, I was willing to oblige.

"Really? And why ever not?" I refrained from adding, "you

big lummox."

"Because," and he leaned towards us as if imparting the wisdom of the ages, "if a sea is rough enough to capsize one of these beauties", and he smacked the edge of the boat, "then it's a sea what can't be swum in anyways. So, it's best not to struggle, and just drown, quick like."

I gulped and held on to the currach very tightly during the rest of the trip.

The beach we landed on was soft and sandy. It was a glorious afternoon, so we walked all over the rocky island – met farmers and fisher folk, had some views of the sea that literally made me gasp with delight. Later, we went to the pub, snuggled up to the fire and told each other stories while we clung to our mugs of piping hot tea. It was truly lovely.

But, His Majesty had been saving a particular treat for us.

"Honoured guests," he announced, "it is time for a drink."

Doris and I were expecting a sherry, or perhaps a nice nip of whiskey, even a brandy if he was being particularly extravagant. But the King had different plans. He went over to the barman, said something in Irish and a bottle was fetched. There was a solemnity to the whole affair that made me think we were in for something.

Rory came back to the table with a bottle with no label, containing a clear liquid. Oh dear.

"Now girls," he said, pulling the cork out of the top of the bottle, "You can't leave my island without a taste of the mother's milk."

As soon as the liquid hit the glass, my eyes started to burn from the vapours. Doris looked as if she had just been asked to swallow a frog.

"Is that what I think it is?" I asked.

"It is if you think it's God's own gift to the Irish." He had filled three small glasses. It seemed unlikely that we could beg for a royal pardon and refuse. Rory lifted his glass and held it to the light. "My own homemade poitín!"

I was no teetotaller, but poitín was something I had managed to avoid my entire life, I would consider it more suitable considered more suitable for cleaning carburettors than for human consumption. The stories I had heard about it were daunting, to say the least.

Rory held out his glass and seemed to be waiting for us to do the same. I glanced sideways at Doris and managed to give her an encouraging nod. We lifted our glasses, clinked them against Rory's with a cry of "Sláinte!", and then watched as he neatly knocked his back in a single swallow. When his head didn't burst into flames, I decided to follow his example, as a polite guest should. I scrunched my eyes shut, tilted my wrist and swallowed it in a blink.

A white-hot poker of meat-devouring heat skewered itself down my throat and into my solar plexus like a lightning strike. Something red and flaming exploded behind my eyes. I think it was my brain.

I heard a whimper and knew that Doris had downed hers as well. As I managed to take a breath and open my eyes I saw her, head back, hands pounding the tabletop. I tried to speak. I think nothing but small blue flames erupted from my lips. Rory looked at us and smiled hugely. Doris was still pounding the table, I was trying to get my eyes back into focus.

"Not bad for your first go, girls," he continued grinning and refilled the glasses. "That was a good warm up."

I tried to say, "Warm up?" but instead I made a sound that was more like a sheep trying to bleat in a way that would be meaningful to a baleen whale.

Rory continued to smile, the twinkle in his eyes looking more and more to me as if they were kindled by the flames from Satan's own soul. Oh, wait a minute, no that was just a lighted match in his hand.

"Now," he said, "Time to learn to drink it properly." He waved the match over the surface of his glass and silvery flames appeared.

He raised the glass, gave us all a big smile and a wink, said something fairly long, yet I'm sure very meaningful, in Irish, and then knocked it back.

The first glass of poitín was already doing a number on me.

"Did you just drink that?" I burbled.

Doris added, "It was on flame ... lighted ... it were burning." She waved her hands.

He passed another lighted match over our drinks.

"It's the best way to have it." He pushed our glasses back at us. "But there's a trick to it."

My immediate thought was – not having a brain might be the best strategy.

He leaned forward.

"Never, ever drink it while it is really on fire." He put one finger up alongside his nose. "Just before you gulp it down, you blow it out – like this."

He picked up my glass and, in what seemed to be slow

motion, he lifted it to his lips, took a deep breath, exhaled across the top of the glass and then gulped it down.

"Thash brilliant," I said.

He refilled my glass and also rekindled it.

"Alright now, lassies," he said, pouring another for himself. "Sláinte!"

I don't remember much of the rest of the day. But the next morning, Doris and I got into the currach to head back to Doolin. Doris had a head on her the size of one of the neighbouring islands. I had to wrap her in a blanket and get her as comfortable as she could get. I felt surprisingly good. Not exactly clear-headed, mind you, but pretty fit, considering.

Rory claimed that I had a good head on me for drink. No doubt, I have an excellent liver also. At any rate, we got back to Doolin and had one last night there of music and then, finally, had to pack everyone up and get back to Dublin. We hated to go but, from then on, whenever we could get away for a day or two, Doolin was the place we would make a beeline for. Sometimes I believe in providence – it was surely a providential gift to stumble upon that magical place.

But, although Luke eventually made music his full-time calling, for the rest of us there were jobs and responsibilities to get back to. I had to get behind the wheel and leave the magical isles behind.

❧❀❧

I kept on at Michels but, with Doris able to do a lot of the driving, we also found ourselves getting very busy with our market business. The Dandelion was always our favourite but there were markets in Cork, Limerick, Galway – and all places in between – so we had somewhere to sell things pretty much every day of the week. It would have been unworkable for just one of us, but with the two of us there was always someone to mind all of the kids while the other either drove or did the selling. I had always enjoyed the selling I did at Michels but the wheeling and dealing we did at the markets was about a million times more fun. And it was no secret that neither Doris nor I were much good at being homebodies.

One Sunday morning, she and I arrived at the street market very early, as usual. Our van was stuffed with a load of goods we knew would have a quick turnaround: packs of toilet paper and kitchen roll, cans of mushy peas that were only slightly dented, assorted dishes and cookware.

As we were unloading, I spotted Annie and Jane across the way. Annie was standing behind a table that had a flowery plastic covering but was otherwise nearly empty. She was trying to arrange a couple of cracked ceramic teapots and a stack of plastic cups so that it would look as if the table were full. Behind her I could see the lank yellow hair of her son, Robert, his head just barely above the back of his wheelchair. Jane was pouring herself a cup of tea from a flask, her hands shaking. She was struggling with diabetes, I knew, and often had bouts where she was tired. But every Sunday she and Annie were there. The extra money was a life-saver for them but, that morning, it was looking a bit bleak.

I wandered over and said hello.

Annie gave me a weary smile, Jane handed me the cup of tea

in her hand.

"Here you go," she said, "Warm ya up a bit."

I handed it right back to her.

"Not at all, I'm warm enough. Let me help you unpack the rest of your things. Hey there, Robert, how are you on this Sunday morning?"

He smiled and shrugged a shoulder – I knew it was his way of waving hello. The muscular dystrophy had left him without much use of his arms but he was always a cheerful fellow, all the same.

Jane set the cup down.

"No worries, we're all unpacked."

I looked at the table. Pathetic didn't even begin to describe it.

When I looked back at Jane she knew exactly what I was thinking.

"The van broke down this week so we weren't able to collect much."

"Could you not even get to Leyden's?"

Leyden's was a wholesaler on the northside. They sometimes offered good deals on bulk items – you weren't going to make as much profit as you would if you sourced it yourself direct but, still, they always had some things you could turn around quickly.

Jane shook her head.

"Well, there's my van right there and we've emptied it. So let's pop over to Leyden's now and get you sorted."

Jane grabbed a handbag from behind the table.

"That's brilliant, Rio, thanks."

Annie grabbed my hand.

"You're very good, thanks a million."

"No problem. Come on, Jane. Let's get over there before all the good ones are gone."

When we arrived, Leyden's was already busy. Lots of traders were there making last-minute buys. I liked to think that I was one of the more savvy ones as I got all of my wholesale buying done during the week. But Jane had not had that luxury, so, while she was examining boxes of washing-up liquid bottles with slightly squashed lids, I was poking around to see what else – and who else – was around.

I noticed that a few folks were buzzing around the stacks of rolls of toilet paper, and I also noticed that Leyden's wholesale price was five pennies higher than what I had paid. I felt rather smug. Suddenly, the feeling was shattered by a clatter of feet and shouting that seemed to roll across the crowd of us like a wave. I turned just as three men wearing black balaclavas shoved their way to the cash registers and jumped on the counters, yelling something about a robbery.

It seemed so ridiculous that, at first, I thought it was some kind of joke. When one of the men started waving a shotgun, I knew I was wrong. The air split with the sound of screaming and, for a moment, I feared being crushed by the panicked mob more than being shot by an idiot with a gun that looked too big for him.

"EVERYBODY DOWN!" The gun-carrying fella screamed, waving the black barrels around in a way that was meant to be menacing.

I fell to the floor in a heap along with everyone else. I lifted my head just a bit to see if I could locate Jane, but couldn't see any sign of her.

While the one fella kept waving his gun around the room, the other two hopped down and forced the cashiers to start emptying their registers into some grubby sacks. None of us knew at that moment that one of the cashiers managed to push the button that was a silent alarm. While the masked men rushed from register to register, filling up bag after bag, the police were already on their way and the nearest Garda station wasn't far.

They hadn't even finished filling the last sacks when we heard the sound of the sirens. Now it was the fellas in the masks who were in a panic.

"Shit! Shit! Shit!" The fella with the gun was screaming.

The sound of the police cars had made everyone on the floor lift their heads and start looking around. This sent the man with the gun into a complete panic.

"Everyone stay down!" He sounded shrill now and didn't seem anywhere near as intimidating as a man with a double-barrelled shotgun should.

As the police started pounding on the doors, the rest of us thought maybe it was time to scramble. The man with the shotgun disagreed.

"I said to stay bloody down!" He was frantic.

When everyone just looked at him, he punctuated his orders by pointing the shotgun at the ceiling and squeezing the trigger. The blast was huge and if anyone had any doubts as to whether he was willing to use his weapon, those doubts were erased. The terror he had meant to instil in us was mollified somewhat, though, by the plaster and powder from the ceiling that then proceeded to fall on his head. He had to waggle his neck to shake the dust out of his eyes and he took a moment to wipe it away from his nose just before he sneezed.

Much as I may have wanted to, I did not giggle. Instead, like everyone else, I went back to lying face down on the floor.

The banging on the doors had become more intense and the robbers gathered together to decide what to do. After a heated exchange, the one with the gun turned and started pointing to people on the floor.

"That one", he would signal with the barrels of his gun, "and that one." The other two would go over and grab the person he had pointed to. They were gathering them all together and I thought – *Are they going to shoot them? What are they doing?*

A phone rang at one of the registers. The girl next to it just stared at it, afraid to move. The man with the shotgun waved both barrels at her.

"Answer it!"

She jumped and grabbed the receiver.

With eyes as big as billiard balls, she whispered into the phone, "Hello?"

After a moment she just nodded and held the phone out.

"It's the police…" she was barely able to whisper. "They want to talk to you."

One of the fellas without a gun walked over and grabbed the phone. He turned his back away from us and we could hear a lot of agitated talk, but I couldn't make out exactly what he was saying. Finally, he yelled something obscene and slammed the phone down. After a few minutes of conversation with his companions, he turned to the crowd of us lying on the floor.

"Listen up!" he shouted. "We've just told the Gards that if they don't let us outta here with the money, we're going to start shooting hostages."

The people they had gathered gasped. One man's knees buckled under him and the woman next to him caught him awkwardly by the elbow. I could hear someone sobbing.

The man with the shotgun spoke up. "We'll need a few more than that."

"Alright." The first fella looked around and reached down and yanked a young man from the ground and shoved him towards the group. Then he reached down for another one – and pulled up Jane.

As he shoved her towards the other hostages I could see her shaking, her lips trembling as she tried not to cry.

I jumped up.

Not a good idea, really. Slow movements would have gone down much better with this lot. Shotgun man went completely bananas.

"I SAID TO STAY DOWN!" I couldn't see under his balaclava, but I suspect he was foaming at the mouth.

I raised my hands like I'd seen them do in the cowboy movies.

"Please, take me and not her. She's sick."

He paused for a moment. The other two men were busy trying to herd all of the hostages off to the other side of the room but they turned to look.

"Wha'?"

"The one there that you just took. She's not well."

Fortunately, Jane was shaking even more when she realised they were all looking at her and that helped prove my point.

The first fella walked towards me.

"How do you know she's sick?"

"She's my friend. She has diabetes."

Behind his balaclava I could see him blink. Apparently, he didn't know what diabetes was, or perhaps it didn't sound serious enough. I tried again.

"And she's appo … eppo … appocoleptic."

I wasn't sure exactly what it was, and Jane had no such thing, but it had what I thought was a very serious ring to it.

He blinked again, but licked his lips in a way that seemed like maybe that had worried him a bit.

The third fella, who had been pretty quiet so far, finally spoke up.

"Jesus, we don't need someone havin' fits or some such. Take yer one there. She looks healthy enough."

So, with an impolite shove, they pushed Jane back towards the group on the floor and the man with the mask grabbed my arm.

I had gone into the store as a disinterested customer. Now, I was a life-at-stake hostage.

They managed to herd us through a back door, into a store-room. Two of them eventually smuggled us out into an alleyway and then into an old rust-bucket of a van. I was crammed into the dirty smelly thing, with all of the doors and windows closed, along with five other panic-stricken people. The two robbers who stayed with us included the one with the shotgun. The third one remained inside the building where he stayed on the phone talking to the police. Some sort of negotiations were going on, but we never knew what they were.

I looked around at the faces of the people inside the van. One woman was crying silently but continuously. The man whose knees had buckled looked pale and greenish at the same time; after about ten minutes he broke into a sweat.

The one with the shotgun was sitting in the front seat, facing his companion who was behind the wheel, but with the gun angled towards us.

I said to him, "Yer man here is going to get sick."

He jerked his head around to look at me.

"Wha'?" The end of the shotgun waggled disconcertingly in my direction.

"He's green at the gills. He's gonna be sick."

The greenish man moaned in what I took to be agreement.

The one behind the wheel turned to look.

"Ah fuck. You need to get him outta here. I'm not gonna clean that up."

The shotgun man snapped back at him.

"I'm holding a fucking shotgun! YOU get him out."

Clearly unhappy, the driver got out and opened the panel door behind me. He reached forward, grabbed the green man by the collar and pulled him out. As he slid past me, I steadied his arm and helped him down and out of the van.

Finding himself in the grip of one of the masked men was enough to put him over the edge and he immediately doubled over and heaved what was apparently a very large, chunky breakfast all over the ground. The man in the balaclava deftly jumped back and managed to avoid spillage onto his shoes.

He yelled a few choice words, then shoved the poor, sick man back into the van and slammed the door shut. As he was opening the door to get back into the driver's seat, I said to the man with the shotgun, "You should get this poor fella a cuppa tea."

He turned to me, the metal barrels pointed right at my face. "Wha'?"

"He's just been sick, he's in a sweat, he needs a cuppa tea."

Spittle came spewing out of the mouth opening of the balaclava.

"A cuppa tea? Am I a fucking caterer?"

His friend was now sitting next to him. He turned towards his partner in arms.

"What is it now?"

"This one thinks we should get the sicko a fucking cup of tea."

The one who had nearly been thrown-up on waved his hand.

"Shoot her."

I don't know who was more surprised – me, or the fella with the gun.

"I'm not gonna shoot her!"

His friend gave him what I can only assume was a terrifying glare – it was hard to tell with all the balaclavas.

"Well, not yet. Not for that."

His shotgun wobbled a bit.

"Not till I get orders to shoot someone."

His friend slammed his hands on the steering wheel.

"We should shoot the whole fucking lot of them and get the

hell outta here."

Several of the hostages gasped – or sobbed – and the man with the shotgun remained silent. The sick man hung his head down between his knees and moaned.

"How about a glass of water?" I asked, in a small voice.

"SHUDDUP!" That came from the two of them at once. I sat back and kept quiet.

Hours went by and the robbers kept shifting around. The one who seemed to be the driver would run back into the store and consult with the third one, and the one with the shotgun would, occasionally, get out and patrol around the van – but he was never more than a step or two away from us.

Once, when he was outside the van, two of the hostages started whispering.

"I need to go to the toilet."

"Oh God, me too. I'm about to burst."

I wish they hadn't said anything. Now all I could do was think about my bladder. When shotgun man got back into the van, there was still some whispering going on. He didn't even look back towards us, he just waved his gun and shouted, "Shuddup!" It had become a reflex.

I decided to speak up, or perhaps it was my bladder that prompted me.

"Any chance we could get a toilet break?"

He turned this time.

"What did I just say? I said SHUDDUP!"

"Okay, okay. It just may get messy back here."

The two barrels moved very close to my face.

"No, one pull of the trigger and *this* will get very messy."

"Alright, alright." I sat back. "It just seems like you fellas have the winning hand, so I don't see what's taking so long."

"What the hell are you talking about?"

"Well, you boys have the money right?"

"Yeah, what if we do?"

"And you have hostages which you haven't hurt at all."

"Yet," he said, rather grimly I thought.

"Well, what have the coppers got on ya then? You give back the money, turn us over safe and sound and all they have ya for is attempted robbery. Easy as pie."

Just then, the driver's door opened and we were joined by our other captor.

"What's all this yapping? Tell them to shut their cake holes." The barrel of the gun wagged a bit in my direction.

"She says we have the winning hand here."

This made the driver turn around.

"Who is 'she'?"

The barrel pointed at me again. The driver gave me a brief look and then turned back around.

"Ah, she's full of shit. Shoot her."

"I'm not gonna fucking shoot her. Yet. She has a point – we give back the money and the hostages and no harm done."

The driver rounded on him.

"NO HARM DONE? We fucking went in there with a shotgun and took their money!"

"But you could give it back," I interjected. "The money hasn't left the premises yet."

The driver reached over and made a grab for the shotgun.

"Give me that thing and I'll fucking shoot her."

Fortunately, his friend was not about to give up his grip. He wrestled it out of the driver's reach.

"Stop that, ya gobshite. Think about it – so far, it's just *attempted* robbery."

"That's a big difference in the eyes of the law", I couldn't help adding.

"SHUDDUP!" They were getting quite practised at shouting in unison.

One of the other hostages nudged me with his foot. When I turned to look at him he shook his head at me. From farther away I heard some soft sobbing and then a trickling sound. A small ribbon of liquid came rolling down the floor.

First vomit, now this. I was afraid of what might be next.

"I'm just saying," said the shotgun guy. "We don't hurt nobody, we don't take no money – we do very little time. 'Cause I ain't seeing no way outta this."

"How do we know they won't throw us in jail and let us rot?"

"You just need a good barrister," I piped up. "I know a fella at the Four Courts, he'd take good care of you."

The shotgun fella looked at me. "Yeah? Do you have his number or..."

"SHUDDUP!"

All on his own, the driver managed to scream so loud I thought the windscreen would shatter.

"Jesus, alright." Then shotgun guy paused a moment.

"What's that smell?"

It was a total of six hours before the third robber came back to the van – followed by a slew of men in uniform. That is definitely the happiest I have ever been to see policemen. Ultimately, though I know it had nothing to do with me, the boys did make the right decision – surrounded, and without any hope of a clean escape, they finally offered to return the money and release the hostages.

After being interrogated by the police and tended to by some medics (mostly they just had to do some rather unpleasant cleaning up), we were allowed to exit through the front of the store. As we headed out, huddled together, a barrage of lights and popping noises rose up in front of us. There were vans and cameras and microphones – a real bloody paparazzi mess.

Some pesky fella with a microphone came up and stuck it in the faces of the first few hostages as they headed towards friends or loved ones who were welcoming them with screams and cries. Each one told him, in one way or another, to bugger off. Everyone was exhausted and just wanted to get home – no one wanted to talk about it. As everyone streamed away, I looked around and saw Jane and Doris waving at me and shouting. As I headed towards them, the man with the microphone edged up to me.

"Have you got anything to say about the experience? It must have been quite an ordeal."

I blinked at him.

"Yes, yes – it's been a long day."

"I know – but it would be great if one of you could talk to us. Everyone else has said no. Please?"

I saw a man with a camera and another guy with a light creeping up behind him. I sighed.

"Sure enough." And I smiled at the camera.

Behind the camera, I saw Doris throw her hands up first in desperation – and then in some hand gestures that were not at all ladylike.

ꙮ

Well, street markets and hostage-taking aside, Doris and the whole lot of us carried on with music as well. That was always a huge part of our lives, no matter what else was going on. One of our favourite haunts was The Embankment in Tallaght, where, after hours, a load of us would gather in 'the office' and the music would go on into the wee hours. Another favourite was The Old Sheiling, in the city. The McCarthy brothers, Mick and Sean, would be there, as well as the likes of Ronnie Drew and Luke Kelly.

It so happened that the owner of The Old Sheiling also owned a pub by the same name in New York City, in the Bronx. One summer, Sean McCarthy organised for a group of us – including Doris and myself – to go over and do an Irish show at The Old Sheiling in the Big Apple – five nights a week, for eight weeks, a dinner show of music, stories and dance.

I had never set foot in America before and New York City was dazzling. I considered myself to be a city girl and I thought, well, New York is just another big city, right? But the sheer size of it, and the energy of it, knocked me off my feet from the first minute. There's a constant hum in the place, a throbbing of humanity and commerce that saturates everything. It's such a vital, invigorating atmosphere, so different from the leisurely pace at home. But, what can I say, everywhere you go people seem to love the Irish and especially in New York. Everyone made us feel welcome and at home. We settled in, organised our evening entertainment of songs, stories and dancing and had them packed in every night.

Besides some singing, one of my main jobs was story telling. Every evening I would tell some stories about the leprechauns and the fairy folk and Tír na nÓg and what not. I would start with some story that I remembered my granddad telling me but then my imagination would always take wing and I would start ravelling some completely new tale that just seemed like a good one at the time. Quite often, I would start with some idea – "There was once a dragonfly that wanted to be a real dragon…" – and just keep going, not really knowing where it would end. It always went down a treat but, after a few weeks, we started getting repeat customers and they would ask me to retell a story they had heard before and, there I was, unable to remember a word of it. Once the story was told, it was out of my head completely. Still, when they asked, I would start again and try to tell a story that had some resemblance to what I had made up the time before. No doubt I quite often left them baffled, wondering why the 'genuine' Irish folktale had mutated into something completely different.

It wasn't all work. We had evenings off and we used them to enjoy the New York night life. One night in particular, we all ended up in – of all places – an Irish bar. Wouldn't you think we'd had enough of Irish bars? But, I guess we just couldn't resist the idea of being the real Irish people in the place. Doris and a couple of the others had figured out that being Irish was generally good enough to get a free drink almost everywhere they went.

The place we went to that night was no exception. As soon as they heard our accents, the big blokes drinking at the bar, who claimed to be Irish American, bought us all drinks and wanted to chat about the 'old country'. As usually happens, the topic got onto the legendary capacity that the Irish are supposed to have for drinking. A couple of the fellas in our group began the customary – and expected – bragging as to how much they could imbibe. The Americans accepted it, good-naturedly.

But then one big fella, named Ray, decided that this unsubstantiated claim to the bragging rights was not satisfactory.

"Hey, Bill!" He called out to the barman. "Bring out the bottle of the good stuff."

There was a hush in the bar. Everyone but us seemed to know what this meant.

The barman appeared with a dingy bottle of clear liquid. *Oh, no.*

"Now, we separate the men from the boys!" Ray lifted the bottle.

"We got us some real po-cheen here. And I'm betting," he looked around at the Irish lads, "that none of you can out-drink me with this."

Ray was about six foot four and weighed close to twenty stone. Judging by the looks on the lads' faces, they did not disagree with him.

"Aw, come on!" Ray reached into his pocket, pulled out his wallet and slapped five, $20 bills on the bar. "I got a hundred dollars says I can out-last you bog trotters at your own drink."

The lads were eying the cash but still not stepping up to the task. They were Irish, after all, they *knew* what drinking poitín could do. The next thing I knew, there were hands shoved in my back and Doris was pushing me forward.

"She'll take the bet!"

Ray and the lads turned to look as Doris pushed and pulled me to the front. Ray looked amused at first. Then, when the other American fellas started to snigger, he looked very annoyed. It was not a pleasant sight to see Ray annoyed.

I whispered to Doris "What the fuck are you doing?"

"Rio, you can do this."

Now I was nose-to-navel with Ray. He towered over me. I think if he could have squashed me with his boot heel, he would have.

"You?" he snarled.

Well, I didn't need that kind of attitude from a big meat-head such as himself. He had called us bog trotters, that could not go unanswered.

"That's right," I said, and gave him my biggest grin. "Don't worry," I nudged him with my elbow, "I'll go easy on ya."

More sniggering followed. I heard the lads behind me saying something but Doris told them to shut up and that she knew what she was doing. Well, I was glad *she* knew what she was doing. There was no graceful way for Ray to back out of it now. The barman brought us two small glasses and filled them with the clear liquid that looked to me like something that could very likely dissolve a human skull.

I reached for my glass.

"Oh no." Ray pulled the glass away. "Not yet."

He produced a lighter and set the surface of his drink on fire. All of his companions, and most of the rest of the bar, gasped and then hooted and hollered.

"My hundred dollars," he announced, "says this little gal here can't drink it like this."

He raised the glass, gave me a shit-eating grin, and downed it. His face turned a bit purple but he raised the glass again and the bar erupted with shouts and claps.

He eyeballed me and then flicked his lighter and set the top of my drink alight.

"That's part of the rules," he said. "The po-cheen has to be drunk the real Irish way."

He turned to his friends. "It's all over now, boys."

Someone behind me said, "Rio, you don't have to do this," but Doris shushed him.

I kept my eyes on Ray and never blinked. I picked up my glass, drew a deep breath and, ever so quickly, blew the flame out, then knocked it back and slapped the empty glass on the bar with a crack.

I grinned at him again. His friends were stunned for a moment and then started laughing and slapping him on the back.

"You're in for it now, big guy," they were saying. I reached for the one hundred dollars.

Ray's hand snapped out like an irate turtle.

"Oh no you don't. I got another hundred bucks says you can't do that again."

The rest of my Irish gang was behind me, especially now that they had seen that I had not burst into flame, fainted or started babbling like a drunken idiot. Yet.

"Come on, Rio – sure, you can do it!"

The entire bar seemed to have turned into a stadium and Ray and I were the match of the day. So be it. Game on. The Americans would slap money on the bar, the barman would pour, Ray would light the drinks and then we'd both knock them back to a tumult of shouts and cheers. At some point, someone asked me if I wanted to sit down but I knew that would be a mistake. No, it was to the last man (or person) standing. If I didn't remain on my feet, I knew I would never be able to get back on them.

Ray, no doubt, thought he would have me after two – maybe three – but we got to five and he had beads of sweat on his forehead.

We got to six and his hand was starting to wobble when he ignited the poitín.

By eight, he had to have one of his friends do it.

Finally, there was nine hundred dollars on the bar. It seemed appropriate, as I felt like I had about nine hundred living brain cells still left in my head. At the most.

Keeping my eyes locked on Ray's sweaty brow, I knocked back number nine. Our glasses cracked on the table. I tried to give him my usual smile which, by now, felt a bit lop-sided and I think I was drooling a little.

As everyone cheered and someone started chanting, "Number ten! Number ten!", it seemed like the world was melting a little bit. No, it was Ray.

One minute he was standing there, still gripping his empty glass after slamming it onto the bar, the next thing, he was sliding down to the ground in a slow-moving avalanche, like an ice-cream cone next to a radiator. There was a thud, and then there he was – in a heap, at the feet of his loyal supporters.

A huge yell went up, mostly from my Irish group. There were lots of cheers and shouts and back-slapping. Doris was keen enough to realise that they had better not slap *me* on the back. No telling what that would bring up. She came around to me and started to scoop up the money.

"Hold up!" It was Ray's mate, and he seemed to be taking charge now that his huge friend was basically a puddle.

"You have to be able to walk out the door on your own two feet. Then the money is yours."

His friends all agreed, noisily.

I looked at Doris. "Give the money to one of our lads. You go outside and wait for me by the door."

"You sure?" she asked. I nodded. My head felt very wobbly. I looked at Doris and realised that she had three eyes in the middle of her forehead and her mouth was upside down. I made a mental note to discuss that with her later.

She headed out the door and I turned to the American lads.

"Right! I'm off now. Thanksh for the drink."

I tried to give what I thought was a jaunty wave. I stepped away from the bar carefully, not wanting to tread on Ray. He was curled up on his friend's feet. I wasn't sure, but it looked like he was also sucking his thumb.

"Before you go…" his friend put his hand on my arm. "Where did you learn to drink like that?"

I grinned and put one finger on the side of my nose.

"From the King!" I announced.

Still grinning, I turned and headed for the door out to the pavement. It seemed to be about a mile and a half, but I knew I had to get to the door, open it and then walk outside or all that lovely money would go right back into those American pockets. Lift one foot, now the other, I kept telling myself. My God, the door didn't seem to be any closer.

As I passed one of the onlookers sitting at a table, he turned to his friend and I heard him say, "She learned how to drink flaming po-cheen from Elvis?"

I couldn't take the time to explain to him the nuances of the King of Inis Oírr. I just kept putting one foot in front of the other, then negotiated the door handle, then I was outside.

I heard an eruption of screams and shouts – and groans – from inside the bar and knew that it was over. I had made it.

Doris came up and took me by the elbow and, boom, my knees buckled and I went straight to the pavement.

I don't remember anything that happened immediately after, but I am told that our lads came out, I was carried to the flat where we were staying and they tucked me in.

I remained tucked in and asleep (some might say, 'passed out') for three days.

But, as they say, the show must go on. As soon as I was back on my feet, it was business as usual.

One evening, a fella came into the bar to see the show and it was obvious that he was not your ordinary punter. He was accompanied by two, huge brutes who shadowed him constantly. The man himself was a smallish fella with thinning hair but wearing an impressively expensive suit. One of the big brutes sat at the table with him but never ate or drank – he just constantly scanned the room. The other took up a strategic position near a back wall, where he could eyeball everyone who came in.

I saw other folks at nearby tables looking at yer man and whispering but no one dared approach him. The brute at the table with him had a bulge under his jacket that I did not think meant that he was happy to see anybody.

We did our show, as usual, and our important guest enjoyed it immensely, hooting and clapping and joining in on some of the songs. He was a fine singer himself.

At the end of the show, he came up to us – with one of the brutes at his shoulder, looking at us the same way that exterminators look at beetles just before they set off bug bombs – and went on and on about how much he had enjoyed it. He asked if we had had our dinner yet.

Sean said no, and that was it, our exalted guest insisted on buying full dinners for all of us. Some tables were pushed together and he sat down with us, while we scraped our plates and sloshed our beer. Though not an Irishman, he loved the music and the lore and was an absolute expert in how to have a good time. More songs were sung as we sat around the table and many, many jokes were told, while the two brutes stood like statues, looking as sour as when they had first come in.

Finally, the dinner ended and, in the wee hours, it was time for our genial guest to take his brutes and go. Before he slipped away, I remembered what Ronnie Drew had told me and I managed to get close enough to him to say a word of thanks.

"That was very kind of you to get us dinner," I managed to say, before one of the brutes could mistake me for an assassin or possibly a ninja.

He turned back to me, blue eyes twinkling, and said, "Hey babe, not at all. Had a great time – thanks to all of you for a really great evening."

"No, no", I said. "Thank *you*, Mr Sinatra."

He winked and then his brutes whisked him away.

ﻬﻬ

The fairytale of New York ended all too soon and it was time to return home. I had to get my feet on the ground and my head back into my business.

I'm a strong-willed person but I have to say that the whole hostage experience put me off street trading just a bit. For a good while, Doris and I had been noticing that there were some fellas driving lorries who were selling things in bulk to us street traders, and our hunch was that the bulk selling was where the real money was.

My ordeal at Leyden's was enough to get me seriously interested in looking into taking our enterprise a step further – which would mean that Doris and I would become lorry-driving wholesalers ourselves. It turned out that from a money-making perspective, we were spot on. That was definitely where the biggest profits were, with the quickest turnaround. These fellas travelled all over – to England, France and Germany – and bought direct, without the mark-up we were having to pay. Our profit margin would definitely go way up and, for a couple of struggling young mothers, this seemed ideal. There was only one problem.

Women couldn't be lorry drivers.

That's what we were told. The Republic of Ireland would not let a woman take the Heavy Goods Vehicle (HGV) license training, let alone the actual test. When I informed Doris about this obstacle to our ambitions, she came up with an elaborate plan that would have permanently effected the reproductive abilities of every man in the entire motor vehicle department – and resulted in some other interesting anatomical changes as well. Unfortunately, it wasn't a workable plan that would actually help us get licensed.

My own opinion was that I had never heard such a load of bollocks in all my life. I got on the phone and talked to everyone I could think of who knew anything about driving lorries or getting a license, and I kept coming up against the same wall. Then it occurred to me that I lived on an island with *two* licensing agencies. The Republic wasn't our only option.

Again, I made some phone calls to Northern Ireland and asked my usual questions – the big difference being, the answers I got were not 'No'. They seemed genuinely un-amazed that I was looking to get myself and Doris licensed to drive big trucks – it turned out there were already some women with HGV licenses in the North. There, the barrier had already been broken.

But there would be a problem with training. Neither Doris nor I could spare weeks on end going back and forth to Belfast to take the courses. We needed to come up with another alternative and that's where my da came in.

He had been running a construction business for years and had loads of fellas who drove lorries for him. Between the two of us, Da and myself called in a few favours and, the next thing I knew, Doris and I were ready to embark on what was virtually a private driver's instruction course for the two of us. We would meet with the fellas a couple of evenings a week and they would let us drive the lorries around a farmyard or a carpark or an open field somewhere. They put us through our paces pretty thoroughly.

I didn't do too badly because, while growing up, I had spent a lot of time around trucks. For Doris it was a bit more alien, not to mention that she got a bit distracted if the driver was the least bit cute. But, after a few weeks, our volunteer instructors deemed us ready to give the test a go – or perhaps they were just sick of us grinding their transmissions. Either way, we were cut loose and we scheduled our tests.

On the day I took my test, I had to squeeze the steering wheel tightly just to keep my hands from shaking themselves to bits. I had come into the thing feeling confident but then I saw the course they wanted me to drive. It was dotted with big, orange traffic cones and signs with arrows and warnings and a curlicue path that was painted on the asphalt. Apparently, I was supposed to navigate the rig I was driving through *that*.

Bloody hell. This was nothing like going around a carpark.

The evaluator sat next to me and instructed me to head out and start weaving around, following the white line. Occasionally, he would tell me to stop and reverse or make a sharp turn, or some such.

The first time I took a corner, I heard a thump and a slight crunch and out of the rear view mirror I saw an orange cone go rolling away.

Shit. I figured that meant that I had already failed. Out of the corner of my eye I definitely saw the man write something on his clipboard.

We kept going and he asked me to pull into one painted area, then reverse the rig and swing it around. As I did so, I saw a little flurry of orange cones skitter away behind me.

I thought my hands were going to shake so hard that they would fly off the steering wheel and the gear stick, completely out of my control. But, somehow, I clung on. Sweat was starting to trickle into my left eye but I didn't dare let go of anything to reach up and wipe it away.

Finally, we were done with the course and we pulled over while he gave me his assessment.

He didn't say anything, just kept ticking boxes and scribbling notes. He wrote in what seemed like a furious scribble on a smaller piece of paper, tore it loose, and handed it to me.

"There ya go," he said, as he handed the paper to me.

The sweat in my eyes made it hard for me to read clearly.

"What's this?" I blurted.

"It's the paper you need that says you passed, so that you can get your license." He started to open his door to get out.

"But … but … I knocked over those cones." I was still blurting.

He waved a hand at me.

"Ah, sure everyone does that."

He shut the door.

Well, double shit with blue balls on top. I was a licensed lorry driver.

Butter. And cheese. We Irish love our dairy products.

For some reason that I have never understood – those of you who need to know can Google it, I'm sure – in the 1970s, the government of the Republic of Ireland decided to tax the bejesus out of dairy products, in particular, butter.

When life gives you lemons, you can use them to make lemonade, or you can get yourself a truck and drive over the border to the North and get cheap, tax-free butter.

It became a popular Sunday excursion for some folks to just pop over the border, tootle around, buy a car-load of butter and then head back home and sell it to friends and family for a modest profit. Then there were those of us with lorries and vans who would bring back huge loads of butter and cheese and sell it for a very healthy profit.

Life handed Doris and I buttermilk and we churned it into a huge supplement to our income.

It wasn't long, of course, before the border officials on the Southern side copped on. They hovered like a cloud of irritated hornets ready to swarm all over us and make us pay their taxes – or be arrested for avoiding them. Every time they figured out where we were getting across, we would find another way to get our golden cargo over the line, tax free. It's the kind of cat-and-mouse game I love. I mean, what do the government types expect? When they create a challenge, resourceful people will rise to meet it.

Over time, it became a sort of generally accepted method of making a few extra bob. I know what the strict letter of the law is, but it was difficult to consider the buying and selling of butter as the purview of hardened criminals. So, it was not a total surprise when, on one of my trips with Doris, we were at our 'supplier's' location (a small dairy farm in County Down) and who should we meet there, also buying butter to take South, but a priest.

We were making a large run. Doris was driving a lorry and I was driving a van. The lorry was ours, the van belonged to some friends on the Northern side who were also interested in making some extra cash.

Doris and I were loading up, chatting away with our friends at the dairy and getting ready to head out. The priest had loaded his boxes into the back of his van, but was shaking like a leaf and had the sweat pouring off him. My guess was that this was not due to an aberrant case of malaria.

I approached him as he was stacking his last box.

"Hey there, Father."

He nearly jumped out of his skin.

"Ah, hello." Fortunately, small women with curly hair and glasses aren't generally very intimidating. He relaxed a bit.

"Everything alright?"

He wrung his hands as if worrying an invisible rosary.

"Ah, yes, I think so, I think so. So far, it's all going well."

"You eat a lot of butter down in your parish?"

"Ah now, you know how it is." This made him really nervous.

"Of course, I do. You just don't seem like the smuggling type, if you don't mind my saying so, Father."

"Well, I wouldn't be, now. But my church is in dire need of a new roof and it has been left to me to raise the money. We've been doing everything possible, but I can't be squeezing blood out of a turnip now, can I? So one of my parishioners suggested this." He waved towards the butter then he pulled at his collar nervously.

"It sounded easy. But now that I'm here, I confess that I'm petrified about crossing back over the border."

"Surely, they won't bother a man of the cloth!"

"Oh, now, they will, they will. I will need to be very careful, I would say. So, I've been given directions on a good way to go, but I'm still quite nervous about the whole thing."

He pulled a handkerchief out of his pocket and wiped at his dripping forehead.

"I've half a mind to call it quits. It's just too nerve wracking and if I got caught what would my diocese do? The more I think about it, the more I think this is a very bad idea."

"Nonsense." I patted him on the shoulder. "You've come this far. Look at that van, Father, that's your new roof sitting in there. Follow Doris and me, we'll get you safely to the other side and over."

His troubled expression changed to, well, I wouldn't say happiness, but certainly less troubled. We arranged ourselves into a sort of convoy with Doris leading the way in her compact lorry, me driving the white van that belonged to my friends in Antrim, and Father Bledsoe in his battered green van carrying the hopes, dreams, and the soon-to-be non-permeable roof of his parish, behind me.

We headed south.

After just a couple of miles down the meandering track that would get us over the border, well away from the noses of any interested parties, I looked in my rear-view mirror.

There was no sign of the green van.

I slowed down a bit to give him a chance to catch up. Still no sign of him. I slowed some more. Still nothing.

Shit.

The lorry was well away in front of me.

We didn't have mobile phones in those days, so I was stuck there with no way to let Doris know what I was doing.

I pulled over onto the verge as far as I could and waited. And waited.

Jesus, it was five long minutes before the pokey, little green van finally showed up. The panicked priest nearly drove into me, though at the speed he was going it would have been barely noticeable.

I hopped out of the van and went to his window. As he rolled it down I could see he was still sweating and his hands were shaking. Saints preserve us, I thought to myself. Although, to be fair, since it was a priest, the saints should have already been well onboard.

"Father, you need to keep up now. We can't be dawdling along here."

"Oh, sorry, sorry. I just don't want to be caught for speeding."

I had to blink and take that in for a second.

"Speeding? Speeding is the least of your worries, Father, if you don't mind my saying so."

He looked at me, goggle-eyed.

The poor fella was just too rattled to think clearly, that was plain.

"Alright now, I will start again and you need to keep right up behind me." I peered at him over the top of my glasses. "I promise I will not drive fast."

He nodded gratefully. "Very good, very good – thank you for that."

Just as I headed back to my van I heard a grinding sound. There was Doris, reversing her lorry to get to where my van was parked.

I ran over to talk to her. She looked decidedly unhappy.

"What are the two of you doing? We need to keep moving."

"I know, I know, but yer man there is panicked and won't drive fast."

"Fast? My granny drives faster than he does."

"Your granny is dead!"

"Exactly. And she still has him beat."

"Look, I told him he needs to keep up. I'm going to drive slower and he'll be fine."

Doris popped her lorry into gear.

"The three of us toddling along at a snail's pace will be a disaster. I'm going on – if you two can't keep up, you're on your own. You know the way."

I stepped back from her door.

"Fair enough. I'll see you over there."

The gears ground a bit and then she was away.

I waved at Father Bledsoe, got back in my van and away we went.

'Away' being a rather euphemistic term for our timid advance towards the border. No matter how slowly I went, he seemed to go slower. I kept looking in the rear-view mirror, trying to keep him in sight, and he would constantly fall back till I would have to come to a near standstill to wait for him to catch up. I suppose his knees were shaking so badly he couldn't keep his foot on the accelerator.

Doris was long gone before us.

It was up to me to drag this poor, quaking, would-be smuggler safely across the border and past the customs officials lurking on the other side.

There were no markings on the little track we were using, so Father Bledsoe couldn't tell when we had crossed from the North to the South. But it would have been of little consolation to him – we wouldn't be safe until we were about ten miles into the South, well past the customs station in Dundalk.

Once we turned off the track and onto something more like a real road, I thought the priest's panic would leave him and we could drive at a more respectable pace.

I was wrong.

He continued to dawdle like he was a sloth lounging in a tub of low-temperature marmalade. I kept having to resist applying some decent pressure to the accelerator and it was making my leg ache. I had to spend as much time looking in the rear-view mirror to see if the priest was behind me as I did looking through the windscreen and I was getting a crick in my neck. And, of course, Doris was long gone, so I would be on my own for the rest of the trip. All in all, it was not the best of times.

I gently applied the brakes again and, around the corner behind me, I saw the green nose of Father Bledsoe's van creeping forward.

Finally.

We seemed to be inching our way down the road, which was worrisome as it wouldn't be long before traffic would build behind us, getting irritated by two vehicles sluggishly worming their way along curvy stretches of the road where they could not be overtaken. I was starting to sweat a little myself.

If we had gone just another two miles, we would have made it to the nearest village and been swallowed into the normal traffic. But, out where we were, on a quiet road that didn't go to much of anywhere, two vans crawling along like a couple of pensioners on rusty roller skates was just too obvious.

Sure enough, they swooped down on us from out of nowhere and had likely been following us for a while.

I think they nabbed us primarily because they were sick to death of the bloody creepy-crawling. I could just imagine the two customs men in their surveillance van saying, "Bugger this, I want to arrest someone before my teeth fall out."

At any rate, the next thing we knew there were sirens and a Garda van and some customs cars swarming all over poor Father Bledsoe (who, amazingly, did not pee himself) and me – our vans of 'contraband' were hauled off to the customs depot in Dundalk.

We were asked why we had so much butter. They directed their questions at Father Bledsoe. Apparently, he looked like a ringleader and I was a mere accomplice. I decided to let them find out for themselves that the poor man couldn't have led a ring of Ring-a-Ring-o'-Roses.

Father Bledsoe did not disappoint.

"Alright now, Father, do you mean to say that this one hundred and sixty pounds of butter in the van you were driving was for your personal consumption?"

The priest's eyes were bulging and his collar was soaked with sweat.

"Grrrggghh," was all he managed.

One of the customs men, who I thought of as 'Frog Face', acted as though that was an intelligent answer. Perhaps, in his range of experience, it was.

"Now, Father," he said and crossed his arms. "That seems like an awful lot of butter for one person, all at one time, don't you think?"

Poor Father Bledsoe. Everything he had feared had come to pass. All he could think about was the trouble he was going to be in with his diocese. He was thinking that being caught as a smuggler was going to mean the end of his tenure at his parish, the end of any hopes he had for advancing in the Church – it might even mean the end of being a priest. His whole life was crumbling before his eyes and these interrogators wanted to ask him about how much butter he ate.

He appeared to give the entire situation a great deal of consideration, mopped his brow (again) and replied.

"Blrrrrrrgllll."

Then he started to weep.

Frog Face was a hard man. I expect making priests cry was all in a day's work for him. He turned to me.

"So."

I blinked back at him. There was a long silence.

He tried again.

"So."

He was expecting the awkward silence to make me blurt

something. I was blurt-less.

He tried another tactic. He stood up and started pacing around the room. The other customs man, for whom the nickname, 'Mouse', seemed apt, remained seated and silent.

"One hundred and sixty pounds of butter in the green van, and two hundred and twenty in the white van."

He leaned over his desk and glared at me.

"Do you have a tax receipt for any of it?"

Father Bledsoe blew his nose into his sweaty handkerchief. Frog Face turned his glare in the priest's direction.

"Well? Any receipts?"

I was afraid that the priest would clear all the snot out of his head and say something intelligible – and incriminating – so, I decided to speak up.

"Don't we get to make a phone call?"

Frog Face was not happy. He looked at Mouse, who shrugged and nodded.

"Yeah, yeah – you get to make a phone call."

"I think we can make some calls and get this all straightened up." I leaned over to the Father. "Isn't there someone in your parish you would like to call?" I grabbed his wrist so he would look at me. "Someone who knows you're here?"

I was hoping he would take the hint that he should call whoever it was who had helped him organise coming North to collect the butter, as perhaps they might be helpful in extricating him from this mess. Otherwise, I was afraid he would panic and do something useless, like phone his Bishop and tell him everything. This was no time for confessions – of any kind.

Meanwhile, I made a call of my own. The customs men were listening, so I had to be careful. I suppose they thought I was calling for legal help, or for someone to bail me out if it came to that. But I called my friends in the North who owned the van I was driving.

"Hello, this is Rio. Yes, my friend the priest and I were driving our vans – the white one and a green one – and got pulled into the customs station here at Dundalk. Yes, it would be great if you could come down here and help get it sorted. Thanks."

I hung up the phone and smiled at Frog Face.

"They said they will be here in an hour."

"To do what?"

"To get it all sorted." I smiled again and asked if I could get a cup of tea for the priest.

Frog Face and Mouse decided they were happy enough to let us stew for an hour. They might get proof that the taxes had been paid, or more likely they would be able to book us, confiscate the butter and charge us a huge fine. Either way, things were looking good for them.

Meanwhile, I also knew that before too long things would definitely get sorted, one way or another. My friends who owned the van were very possessive. And they wanted their van back. With the butter.

An hour went by.

Mouse and Frog Face had dumped the priest and me in a busy room full of desks and phones and people running about. We were plonked onto a couple of wooden chairs against a wall with lukewarm, weak tea in plastic cups and left to wait. We were waiting for our salvations, each in our own way.

He had found his rosary beads and murmured over them in between noisy bouts of nose blowing. He was too distraught to talk to me. I never found out who he had called and I did not want to tell him that I was getting things sorted for us both. There were too many other ears around and I wasn't exactly sure what was going to happen.

After the hour had come and gone, Frog Face came in to check on us.

"Where are these people who are supposed to sort this out?" Frog Face still thought that the priest and I were partners in crime, so he directed his glare at the Father.

An hour of nose blowing had not helped his nerves. A confrontation with the uniformed man sent him into an emotional tailspin.

"Plrrrrgnnn?" was the best he could do.

Frog Face turned his glare to me.

"Sure, these things take time. They'll be along soon." I smiled at him. "Might be they got caught in traffic."

No doubt that made Frog Face concerned that whoever was coming along to help was the same sort of driver as the priest. In which case, we would all be there till Christmas.

"They had better get here soon or the two of you will be spending the night in a cell."

He snarled and left us to our lukewarm tea.

Another hour went by and I could see Mouse and Frog Face conferring out in the hallway and looking through the glass in the door to where Father Bledsoe and I were sitting. Frog Face was agitated. Mouse was ominously quiet and would stare at us with brown, unblinking eyes.

Frog Face had just put his hand on the door handle and was about to come in and probably drag us off to the dungeons, when there was an incredible uproar throughout the building. A siren was wailing somewhere outside and a slew of people came tearing through the hallway. Someone in a uniform ran up to Frog Face and yelled a lot of unintelligible things with big arm gestures, and then the two of them went running off. Phones were ringing and people in the room were walking quickly in and out, back and forth, and people were running to the windows and looking and pointing.

Eventually, they started turning and taking furtive looks at myself and the priest. They did not look happy.

When the tumult finally died down, it was Mouse who came to see us. He just stood in front of us for a moment, arms folded, looking.

"Come with me."

He turned and left the room and the Father and I followed along. The poor priest had such trembly knees they were practically knocking together as we went down the hallway back to the room where we had been interrogated. Frog Face was already there.

When he closed the door behind us I knew we were in trouble.

"Okay, you smart arses, where are they?" he thundered at us, threatening to pop his bulbous froggy eyes right out of their sockets.

"Glllbrrrbb!" Father Bledsoe collapsed into a chair in a heap.

"You!" Frog Face came right at me with a finger stabbing into my face. "Who did you call?"

Like I was going to tell *him*.

"What's this all about?" I turned away from him and looked at Mouse.

He kept his oval, brown eyes in an unblinking, rodent stare.

"We have a bit of a problem." At least he was remaining calm.

"Is it your problem or my problem?"

Frog Face nearly leapt over his desk. "Don't you be a wise arse with me!"

I kept my eyes on Mouse.

The corners of his mouth, where his bristly whiskers should have been, crinkled into a rueful smile. He shrugged.

"Where are the damned vans?" Frog Face had grabbed Father Bledsoe by the front of his shirt and was shaking him. It caused a new eruption of gurgles. And snot.

"Leave him alone! We've been sitting in here for two and a half hours, how would we know where you put our vans!"

"Ahermm." That was Mouse clearing his throat. He then gave Frog Face a look that would curdle milk. Or perhaps melt butter.

Frog Face let go of the priest.

"We don't have your vans." Mouse almost mumbled it.

"You what?"

Frog Face slammed his hand on his desk.

We don't, SLAM, have, SLAM, your fucking vans! SLAM.

"Whaaarrrllppp?" Father Bledsoe had perked up a bit.

Mouse scratched behind his ear. He used a finger but I bet,

when he's alone, he uses a hind foot.

"Some uniformed men entered the carpark and left with your vans." He scratched again. "We now have reason to believe they were not actually … ah … hrrmm … officials of the customs department."

"Are you telling me that my van, and the van that belongs to the Father here, have been stolen from a government customs office carpark?"

Now, it was Frog Face's turn to mumble. "Eh, yeah…"

"This is outrageous." I wanted to dance a jig around the room but, in a feat deserving of a little golden statue, I kept the expression on my face stern.

"It certainly is." Mouse had a cold anger about him.

"Well, what happens to us now? Are you going to press charges, or what?"

Mouse really bristled at that. "No, obviously we can't. We have no … evidence."

"So, we are free to go?"

"Yes." Mouse looked at me very strangely. "You can both go."

Frog Face slumped into the chair behind the desk and thumped a fist on it. But he had nothing to say.

"Come on, Father. Let's call a taxi and go home."

Mouse stuck out his hand.

"Oh, no. No taxis for you. You can walk."

"But we need to get this man back to his parish."

The whisker-less Mouse twitched again. "That's unfortunate but, given the security concerns we have here, it is the best we can do."

Frog Face punched the desk again. "Just be glad you're getting outta here at all. If it were up to me we would skin the likes of you alive. Now get out."

No need to ask me twice. I pulled the priest to his feet and we walked out. "Luuuurqf!" Father Bledsoe raised his hands and his eyes as if to thank heaven for his deliverance. I knew better. A few hours later, we were in a car meandering up a winding track of a road, back the way we had come from earlier in the day. The driver took us off onto what looked like a cow path and we stopped at a half-fallen-down barn behind a stand of trees.

There were the vans.

Father Bledsoe had his van and butter returned intact, along with a map showing him a way to get home that went nowhere near Dundalk. Meanwhile, my load of butter had been transferred into a red saloon car. The white van would stay in the barn for a while, until the customs folks had stopped looking for it.

My partner in crime drove away, map in hand, and I never heard from him again.

My friend handed me the keys to the red saloon car with a wink.

"Better luck this trip now, Rio!"

"I hope so!" I laughed and took the keys. "By the way … nice shirt. You look good in a uniform."

"No, I don't. It's ugly as hell."

"Well," I said, "be grateful you don't have to wear it all the time. Or we'd have to start calling you Frog Face."

He gave me an odd look, I started the car and then was back on the road.

Part Three

Raise the Children Well
France, 1970

The asphalt trembled under the lorry wheels and the gear stick shuddered comfortably in my left hand. The sky was a streaky blue, driving conditions were good, and just a few miles ahead was one of my favourite cafes.

I loved these lazy, long hours. The busy part of the work was over now, all that remained was to haul the twenty-foot trailer home. A stop for a bite to eat, some strong coffee and a chat with Adelle, then a straight shot to Le Havre where I'd board the ferry home.

I slowed at a small junction and changed down through the gears as I turned the lorry around a bend in the road to the right. A middle-aged Frenchman, his small dog on the end of a lead, a newspaper under his arm, had looked up as the whining engine breezed past him. When he saw my curly head smiling at him from the cab window, the poor man nearly dropped everything – his jaw especially.

I nodded at him, still grinning toothily. The man's look of petrified horror at seeing a woman behind the wheel was delicious. I would savour it for the rest of the drive into Sainte Ramone.

Ah, but the time to savour my small triumph was short – there was the cafe and under the striped awning I could see Adelle. She was clearing some dishes and talking to someone, though I couldn't see who.

After parking the lorry next to the only petrol station in the village, I crossed the road and could see a bushy stand of untidy brown hair bristling above a tabletop as Adelle leaned over and handed it a spoon. A tiny hand shot out and I knew who it was. I walked into the shade of the awning and headed for Adelle.

"So, the scamps are back, are they?"

Adelle turned, and shrugged.

"Of course, and they are very hungry."

As I pulled out a chair and sat down, I peered over the table edge. Sitting cross-legged on the ground, bowls in their laps, spoons in their hands, were two of the filthiest children I had ever seen.

"Christ." I hadn't meant to say it in front of the boys but, well, Christ they looked awful.

Adelle wiped her hands on her apron and shoved a basket of bread towards the sound of the soup being slurped.

"I know," she said. "It is very bad this time. They came not for the begging of money but for food. They don't know where their maman is."

I picked up two rolls from the basket and handed them to the boys. They were snatched so quickly it was like being snapped at by sharks.

I leaned down to the older of the two – I couldn't pronounce his name so I just called him Jackie.

"So, how are yas gettin' on?"

Jackie looked back at me, blankly, and kept chewing. His face was shiny with dirt, his clothes soiled and crumpled and emitting a ferocious smell.

His younger brother gazed at me briefly and I was shocked to see that his eyes were gooey and crusted. He blinked very hard and then coughed: it was a thin cough that sounded like pebbles dropped in a dusty jar, it was as if he didn't have the strength to come up with enough phlegm for a proper cough. Something about the fevered, feeble timidity of it scared me.

Adelle seemed to have felt it, too.

"The little one, he is sick. I think it might be bad."

I grabbed two more bread rolls and handed them to Jackie. Without a pause, he stuck one in his mouth and handed the other immediately to his brother.

I smiled. That was why I had always liked them. They were obnoxious little buggers sometimes, hanging about the cafe begging for small change. They weren't above reaching into a handbag or a pocket, either. But it was always only change they were after, they were not dedicated thieves.

Their mother, lolling at home in her alcoholic stew, had ordered them to go out and bring back change and that is what they did.

At seven years old, and with a brother to care for, Jackie was unable to do anything beyond what he had been told to do. He brought home the change and he kept his brother as fed and safe as he could.

Over the past few months, I had known it was a bad situation, but something had changed.

"How long have they been like this?"

Adelle wiped her hands on her apron.

"I am not sure, perhaps a week? I did not know until two days ago that they had nowhere to sleep. Last night I let them sleep in the shed."

I didn't speak much French but decided to try a little.

I leaned down to Jackie.

"Where est la maman?"

Jackie looked at me thoughtfully, digesting both his soup and the awful French. He shrugged, waved one hand in a dismissive gesture and went back to his soup. Adelle decided this would take some time, so she sat down next to me.

The only other customers were a couple sitting at a table on the other side of the patio, half-empty coffee cups in front of them, engrossed in a conversation that, from what I had managed to overhear, had something to do with both 'l'amour' and 'le denier'. Always a bad combination.

"They tell me she is not at home and that home is closed. They cannot get in."

"They're locked out?"

Adelle considered that a moment. "I believe it is more. Everything is gone."

"Did their mother take everything and move?"

"Perhaps. I think it was all taken by the landlord. I don't

know what you say in English."

I contemplated Jackie's dirty, bushy head of hair a moment.

"Sounds like they were evicted."

"Ah, as you say."

"And I would also say it seems their mother is a right bitch and has scarpered off without telling them where she went."

Adelle shrugged.

"Well. What about other relatives? Grandma? Aunts? A big, fat, rich uncle?"

"I asked." Adelle gathered up the bread basket. "They don't know of anyone."

I took the bread basket back and handed it to Jackie.

"How long can they stay with you then?"

Adelle stopped halfway to reaching for the basket again.

"They can stay a long time – but it is not good for them to stay in the shed, no?"

I turned to look at Adelle. I am sure that for Adelle it gave her the uncomfortable self-consciousness one would get if caught under a microscope, swimming about on a glass slide roiling with pond scum.

"Is that the best you can do? Let them sleep in your shed?"

"I am sorry." Adelle snatched the bread basket back very decisively. "It is the best I can do."

Settling for winning the skirmish rather than the entire war, Adelle took the bread basket and retreated to the kitchen.

I looked down thoughtfully on the boys' heads as they were scraping out the bottoms of their soup bowls with the last pieces of bread.

"Alors there boys. How about if you come and stay with

your Auntie Rio for a bit?"

Jackie peered up at me, he seemed to be thinking that I had done a really good job getting them that extra bread. He seemed to admire that – it was the kind of sleight of hand he and his brother depended on for survival. He looked up at me and gave his own big cheeky grin right back.

Well, I thought, I'll take that for a yes.

Once we were on the road and the excitement, or the sugar – I had bought the boys some sweets for the trip – had worn off, the boys were delighted to crawl into the bed built into the cabin of the truck. It was above and behind my head on a shelf, hidden behind a hinged drop-down door. An hour and a half later, the truck was in the queue at the ferry landing at Le Havre.

As I drove up to hand over my ticket and papers, I noticed the man's eyes flicker across the front seat. The hinged door over the bed stayed closed and the boys were completely silent. As my papers were put back into my hand and I was waved through, I finally exhaled.

I didn't really know if anyone on the ferry would care if I had two, pint-sized extra passengers. I also didn't want to find out. Once I got the rig squared away, I knocked on the hinged door and swung it open. Jackie looked at me expectantly while his younger brother (what was I going to call him? Adelle had told me his name but it was unpronounceable) seemed a bit drowsy and still had some crust on his eyelashes.

"Come on, you lot! Let's stretch our legs."

Amazing how a tone of voice and the right hand gestures can compensate for language. The boys jumped down and followed me up the stairs to the passenger decks.

When they passed by a large picture window, the boys stopped as if smacked. They stood for a moment in dead silence, then the younger one grabbed Jackie's arm and started babbling excitedly. Jackie was shaking his head and babbling back.

He turned to me, just as his brother's voice was starting to sound hysterical. His eyes were huge.

He asked me something – it sounded, based on my limited French, as if he was asking, "Where?" As in, perhaps, "Where are we?"

Tears were now dribbling down his brother's face, mingling with the crust and the ever-present snot.

It was then that I realised that when Adelle had told the children that they were going to stay with me for a while, that she neglected one very important point.

She had not bothered to mention that my home was in Ireland.

The boys were staring at the expanse of dark, dingy, seemingly endless water with something between terror and disbelief. *Well*, I thought, *this could be interesting*.

⁊❀❀⁊

Bringing home the two French boys only raised a minor flurry in my household. I asked the local priest, Father Neary, to help locate any family that they might have, other than their useless mother. A neighbour spoke very passable French, so we got them all sorted.

Meanwhile, I had been a busy girl in other ways.

The day I gave birth to my second child, I woke up very early with the telltale pains and thought to myself, *I must get down to the shop and make sure everything is in order.*

With my first child, the birthing pains had gone on all day, with nothing much to show for them until the last couple of hours. To me, this seemed like a dreadful waste of time. There were things that needed to be sorted before I got 'confined' again for a few days.

So, heavy on my feet but, otherwise, feeling not too bad, I popped into Michels. I wanted to get the new display up in the window. With First Communion season coming up, I wanted our dresses and veils to make an eye-catching show.

The other girls wouldn't be in for an hour or two, so I had the place to myself. I moved mannequins about, arranged bits and pieces, sorted through some boxes, only occasionally having to stop and take some deep breaths while a contraction skewered through my belly. I was not being careless, I only climbed up a very short ladder to finish draping the gauzy material across the top of the window, which would frame the whole vignette nicely and was well worth it.

I was sorting through some boxes behind the counter when I felt a fiery stab that I thought was going to tear me in two. Now this was different. Having been through the whole ordeal before, I thought I knew what to expect but this was not at all like what I remembered. This had to be a sign that things were moving along – and fast. Thank goodness the window was looking tip-top.

I picked up the phone and rang Doris.

"Yeah, so I will be heading to the hospital soon."

"Ya will?" She somehow managed to sound bleary eyed, I don't know how that's done over the phone, but she did it.

"Yes, the baby's coming."

"Ah, the baby! Christ!" I now heard a flurry of activity at her end that seemed to remove all bleariness.

"So, the window here is done and the cash and receipts are all in order. You have someone to help with the driving, yeah?"

"Sure I do. Are you fixed to get to the hospital? Shall I collect you?"

"Not at all." I reached down and picked up my handbag. Completely unexpectedly a pain shot through me and I made a rather undignified sound into the phone.

"You okay?"

"Yeah, yeah." I had to lean on the counter a moment.

"Anyway, I'll do just like I did last time. I'll drive myself to the hospital."

Doris chuckled a bit.

"Fair enough. Does Hughie know you're heading in?"

"I'll phone him from the hospital. Ooof." Damn, another undignified noise.

"Rio, you don't sound well. I'll come over and collect you and take you in."

"No, no." I buttoned my cardigan as best I could and grabbed my handbag again. "I'm leaving now and I'll be grand. Come and see me in the ward this evening – it will all be done by then."

Before she could argue, I hung up and headed out the door, locking it behind me. As I stepped away to head towards my car, my knees started to buckle.

The first time I had a baby, I had packed myself up and headed to the hospital at the first twinge. It had aggravated the hell out of me that it was ages before anything moved along. So, this time I had decided to wait till I was much further in the process before going anywhere near a hospital. But, now, everything seemed to be racing forward much more quickly than before. It occurred to me that I should probably not be behind the wheel if I was going to double over and make 'ooof' noises every five minutes.

I straightened up and headed towards the kerb. Traffic was starting to pick up and, before too long, I managed to wave down a taxi.

As I waddled towards the car to open the back door, the driver's eyes widened.

I flopped awkwardly into the back seat and pulled the door closed behind me.

"Mater Hospital, please. Ooof." Damn it, there it was again.

"Right away. Looks like you're ready to go there, missus."

I was becoming increasingly disinclined to make small-talk.

"Yes, we should – ooof – hurry."

And then I followed with another "ooof".

"You got it, missus."

We dawdled along for a few minutes and I started feeling a bit better. I sat up straighter and looked out the window.

"Ah, now you should probably go left up here. You don't want to get stuck in the traffic."

I saw his eyes flicker at me in his rear-view mirror.

"Yeah, well we're real close now. It will just be a few minutes."

I settled back and closed my eyes for a minute, thinking the next time I opened them we would be at the hospital. Coping with the contractions was starting to take a lot of my concentration.

I felt the car slowing down and thought we'd made good time after all. It came to a stop and I opened my eyes. The taxi driver was opening his door and getting out, the engine still running.

How chivalrous! He was going to open the door for me. I felt a surge of warm feeling for the dear man, followed by a contraction and an "ooof".

His door slammed shut and I was surprised to see him walking away from the car rather than grab my door handle. I looked around and was horrified to find that we were parked in front of a small shop. I grabbed the handle and opened my door myself and screamed at his disappearing back.

"What the fuck are you doing?"

He turned towards me, while still walking in the direction of the shop.

"Just popping in to get a packet of fags. Won't be a tick."

"Are you fucking mad? I need to go now!"

He didn't even look back but just yelled over his shoulder.

"Don't you worry, won't be a minute."

And off he went into the shop. I couldn't believe it. I sat for a moment and looked around. Jesus, we were still ten minutes from the hospital and the pains were now just a couple of minutes apart.

Well, fuck this. The engine was running and there was still no sign of the driver. So, I scooted myself out of the back seat, opened his door and got behind the wheel. With a quick glance in the rear- and side-view mirrors, I released the handbrake and put the thing into gear.

I can be an impatient driver at the best of times. This was definitely not the best of times.

I wove in and out of traffic, I cursed the car (I think his timing belt needed some adjustments), I cursed other drivers, I cursed the traffic, I cursed the weather (it started to rain and I couldn't figure out how to work his bloody windscreen wipers), and, most of all, I cursed the contractions which had started to make my eyes water.

With my knees feeling like meaty sacks of jelly, I pulled into the carpark at the hospital and stopped the car in a very illegal manner near the entrance. I pulled on the handbrake and yanked the keys out of the ignition. I opened the door and stood up, then immediately doubled over.

I took a few deep breaths and managed to get myself to the reception desk. The lady there took one look at me and immediately whipped around and yelled for an orderly to bring a wheelchair.

I sank into it gratefully.

As the young man started to wheel me to the maternity ward, I waved to him to stop and then beckoned to the lady at reception.

She ran over to me and leaned over.

"Yes, love, what can I do for you?"

I handed her the taxi man's car keys.

"Someone is going to come looking for these." She looked down into her hand and then looked at me.

I waved at the fella pushing the chair to continue on.

Forty-five minutes later, I gave birth to a healthy, cheeky, chubby little boy. We named him Patrick. The next day, I had an interesting conversation with some Gardai who came to visit me in the hospital, looking for a missing taxi...

꩜

It seemed to be the year for babies.

My eldest, Gwen, was just two years old and Patrick was a newborn when my dear friend Mary came to me one day with her announcement.

Mary was twenty-five, had a good job at Arnotts and still lived at home. She had never shown much interest in the local lads that we knew. Her parents were beginning to think she would never get hitched and then she delighted them by taking up with a nice-looking English fella who was working at a betting shop. Nigel was his name. And I never liked him.

Now, I wouldn't have said so to Mary. She was mad about him and it was her first serious case of love, so I let it be. I figured it would run its course, one way or another.

I had forgotten that nature sometimes has a way of making us change course – and nature had definitely had her way.

"I'm pregnant."

She looked down into her coffee cup, sitting on the other side of my kitchen table. I was giving her a fierce look through my glasses but she was clever enough to know not to look up.

"Well. Shall we start picking out the wedding invitations?"

She shrugged.

"I suppose so. He hasn't said anything yet."

"He hasn't said anything?"

"I told him last night. He ... em ... wasn't happy."

"Ah shit, he didn't hit you or anything, did he?" I was ready to go grab a broom handle and give him a talking to myself if that was the case.

"No, no. He's nothing like that, Rio. He just got very quiet. When I asked him what we should do he said he'd have to think about it."

"What a load of bollocks! What is there to think about?"

"His family back in England, I guess. I don't know."

"Well, when you see him tonight you had better explain to him what is expected. He wanted to play house, now he gets to play for keeps."

"Yeah, he knows. It's just not what we had planned, ya know?"

I grabbed her hand and smiled. "No, it never is. But plans can change and still work out."

She smiled back.

The next day she dropped by. I was expecting a bubbly bride-to-be to skip up my stairs. She was stoop-shouldered and her eyes were puffy.

Oh dear.

I set a cup of coffee in front of her on the table.

"So, how's things?"

She sniffed.

Shit.

"Oh, Rio, he didn't answer any of my calls yesterday. I called him at his place and I called him at work."

"The gobshite. Well, we'll go to his place and roust him."

She shook her head. Tears were flowing now.

"I went by there this afternoon. He's … he's …"

That did it. Her shoulders started to shake and the tears flowed down in ribbons of salty grief.

"Oh, Rio – he's gone!"

Double shit. I threw my arms around her.

"Now, now. He probably just needed to get away for a day or two to figure out how to make this all work. I don't know how it is that men do what they do and then seem absolutely gobsmacked when they have to face the consequences."

She was shaking her head.

"No, no. They told me he has completely moved out. He told his landlord he was … he was … going home." This brought a new eruption of tears.

"Home, as in England? He went back to bloody England?"

She nodded, wordlessly.

Triple bloody shit. I sat next to her and put both my hands on hers.

"Look at me."

She blinked back the biggest of the globs and looked up, her lip trembling.

"What do you want to do? Tell me."

"I want to get married and have the baby."

I nodded.

"Fine. We can do all of that except for the getting married bit."

"What?"

"We can't make him come back. He may come back later, of

his own free will but, in the meantime, you need to deal with this, with him or without him. If you want to have this baby then let's have it."

"Let's?"

"Sure enough. What will your parents say when you tell them?"

"Oh, God. Oh, Rio, I think I'm gonna be sick."

I patted her back.

"No, you're not. We're gonna face this and we're gonna make it work."

She gulped. I tried not to think about what she just swallowed.

"My parents will kill me! And then they'll make me give the baby up. I know they will."

I decided not to point out that killing her now would remove all need for adoption.

"Okay, so it's best if they don't know."

Now, she looked at me as if I had been sniffing some paint thinner.

"I don't see how on earth they can *not* know! Hard to miss a big, pregnant woman in the house."

I was running a slew of scenarios through my head. Some were crazy, even for me. But I came up with one that I thought could work. It just could work.

"Alright, now." I took her hand again. "This is what we'll do."

RIO'S SINGLE MOTHER PREGNANCY PLAN

1. Wear loose clothing. Start now and continue on so

that there won't be a sudden change. Make sure that you choose roomy, loose, baggy clothes so that no one can tell how big you are under there. If anyone asks, just say that you like dressing comfortably and then start discussing your painful menstrual cramps in detail. This is an especially powerful deterrent when used with men and acts as a useful diversion with women.

2. Start eating like there is no tomorrow. Every time your parents and friends see you, they should see you stuffing some fattening food in your mouth. Keep biscuits, chocolate and crisps on hand at all times so that you can be gorging on them on the fly.

3. When asked why you are eating so much, start to sniffle and moan about something (see point number 1 for a possible topic). Having the 'blues' is always considered an appropriate reason for overeating.

Mary was a star student. Her parents never suspected a thing. She was one of those lucky women who gained weight but didn't develop an obviously pregnant ovoid shape, so the baggy clothes worked a treat. Also, as the months went by, she managed not to have a pregnant-woman waddle.

In her last few weeks, she kept a suitcase packed and hidden under her bed at home. On the morning when she started having pains, she grabbed her suitcase and told her parents that she was going away on a holiday with me for a week or two.

I collected her and took her to the hospital and she had a lovely, tiny, but healthy, baby girl. She named her Rose. We brought Rose to my house where Mary stayed with her for the full two weeks of her 'holiday', and then she went back home, Rose stayed with me. Mary's parents were delighted that she had got over the eating binges and had started wearing better-fitting clothes again.

I saw a lot of Mary for a good while after that – she came to the house nearly every day and stayed involved in everything her little one did. She never heard a word from Nigel, ever again.

It has never ceased to amaze me that there are people in this world who go out and about like nothing has happened and never make any effort to be a part of the life they created.

Rosie grew up believing that I was her mother. It was many years later, when she finished school and was about to go off to University, when we sat down with her and explained that 'Aunt' Mary was really her mother. This may sound like it should have been an astounding bit of information that could do a child's head in. But you need to remember, Rose grew up in a household in which I had foster children, and neighbour's children, and friend's children, and children I had taken in off the streets, coming and going all the time. I wouldn't say she wasn't surprised, but she had been accustomed to the way I dealt with things. She was also old enough to understand how impossible it would have been for her mother to do anything different.

Above and beyond all of that, she knew that Mary had always loved her and always been there for her.

In the end, children always know what really counts.

❧❀❧

The summer of 1971 was busy.

The little French boys were still living with me but were about to go to Portugal to join their family. Our local parish priest, Father Neary, had been a real life saver. Not only did he speak pretty passable French, but he had helped me organise things with the Salvation Army so that we had been able to track down their aunt and grandmother. Poor things, the women had been frantically trying to find the lads. Their grandmother had found out, somehow, that the mother had scarpered and she had sent for the boys to come and stay with her. And then things got a bit strange.

Not being able to speak French, I had relied on Adelle at the cafe to do the translating for me and I had already seen that she tended to edit what she said. By editing, I mean that she would just leave out big chunks of information that might be important. For example, when she had failed to mention to the two little boys that my home was in Ireland, which I would have thought was rather important. Then, I came to find out that when the police in the French village had called to the cafe looking for the boys for their frantic grandmother, poor Adelle had panicked.

I had given her all of my contact information just in case someone came looking for the lads. The sight of the uniforms, however, apparently made Adelle wonder if perhaps she had been a bit out of bounds letting the boys go off with someone she hardly knew who lived in another country. Not sure where she would stand in the whole thing, she played it safe and told the police nothing. She acted like she didn't know anything at all and they went away.

I suppose I can't blame her for wanting to play it safe but, unfortunately, she also didn't think to contact me and let me know that someone had finally come looking. Although the story had a happy ending, it could have been happy earlier if we hadn't had to spend so much time trying to track their family down. But, all in all, the two of them had a great time in the fourteen months that they lived with me. They went to school, they learned English – with pure Dublin accents, the way it should be spoken! – and made loads of friends.

At my end, I had tried to do everything right – I had reported that the boys were staying with me to Father Neary and to the local police. I made it clear that they were just staying with me until we could find some responsible family members that would care for them properly. When we finally took them back across the water, it was a bittersweet journey, early in the summer. However, after I met their granny and their aunt – the mother's sister who lived with her – I knew that the boys were going to finally get the care they needed. It seemed to me, as I headed back to Ireland, that all was right with the world.

It wasn't more than a couple of months later that it all went to hell.

Things had been tense in Northern Ireland, those of us in the South knew that. We tried to keep our noses out of it but, of course, there was no escaping the effects that the violence had on both sides of the border. But, in August, 1971, the impact became inescapable. Hundreds of men and women were rounded up by the government in the North on suspicion of being members of paramilitary organisations. Through some kind of legal wrangling, they managed to round them up and hold them without trial – with no one able to tell how long they would be held. Meanwhile, many of them had children who were now left with perhaps one parent who couldn't afford to feed them while the main wage earner was locked up – while others were left with no parents at all.

The churches and various folks tried to find ways to get the kids sorted, but they quickly became overloaded and had to look outside their own borders for help.

Father Neary and I had already got to know each other well, dealing with the French boys. I guess I shouldn't have been surprised when the knock on the door turned out to be himself. "Well, Father, come in and have a sit down and a cuppa."

"Thank you, Rio, I will." He looked tense. When he sat down he had the coiled look of a spring that would unleash itself at the slightest nudge. I knew the way he operated – he would sit there and make small-talk and work his way around to the subject and then, finally, ease me into whatever it was he wanted to ask me to help with. I normally enjoy the social niceties as much as anyone but there are days when I just want to get to the bloody point.

"What is it, Father? Something up?"

One of the dogs was already sitting on his feet. He scratched her behind the ears and looked up at me – a faint smile, but not one with any laughter in it.

"You have the right of it, Rio. I need to ask your help. We have a few children from the North who need somewhere to stay for a few days."

"Well, that's not a bother, you know that. What ages are they?

"We're not completely sure – anywhere from toddlers to teenagers."

I nodded.

"Well, we can cope with that around here. Sure, I've got beds for another three, I could take five if I get the kids to double up."

He looked up at me and I saw that he was really tense now.

"It will be a few more than five, Rio, I'm sorry to say. I know it's a lot to ask – but we need you to take in half a dozen – maybe ten."

I don't know it for a fact, but I think the expression on my face must have looked something like a pollywog with constipation.

It made him panic a bit.

"It's just for a day or two! Then we'll get them all sorted to various homes where they can stay longer-term if need be. But we need to get them out of the North, Rio. Between the parents being interned and the stress these kids have been under with all the violence – we just need to get them out, now."

"You do know I only have a three-bedroom house?"

"I do. I know it will be a stretch."

A stretch? I felt like reminding him that I wasn't the one who could feed the hungry masses with a stale loaf and a few scrawny fishes.

He wouldn't give up, I had to give him credit. "It's just for a day or two. These kids need a bed and a hot meal while we get the rest of this sorted, that's all."

I looked around my kitchen, in my mind plotting where I could set up extra cots, wondering who would let me borrow some pillows and blankets, deciding how I could rotate a dozen kids through one bathroom.

My distracted look made the Father think I was trying to find a way to back out. He stood to go.

"Well, it's a lot to ask, I know. Thanks, anyway."

"Hold your horses, Father."

I picked up a piece of paper and a pencil from where the kids had been doing homework at the kitchen table. "Now, tell me what's what and let's get this sorted."

I called Doris and had her gather up as many blankets, pillows and towels as our friends and family could spare. She brought them over in the van. She had also brought some bottles of milk, boxes of cereal and loaves of bread. Bless her, she had called in some favours from all over.

We unloaded everything and the house seemed to be filled to bursting. And we didn't even have any of the kids yet.

"Jesus." Doris was looking around the kitchen and into the hallway. "I just can't see where you're going to put everyone."

"Well, me and Hughie can sleep on the floor. And we'll put some cots out in the lounge. We'll have to feed them in shifts."

"Of course, a couple will come to my place." I hadn't asked her to do that – she wasn't as keen on having strangers in her home as I was. For her, that was a particularly big move.

"Well, there you go. That will be a big help right there." I felt better already.

The next afternoon we had things ready and we waited for

their arrival.

And we waited.

And then we waited some more.

I phoned Father Neary once, but got no answer. So, there was nothing we could do but continue to wait. Fortunately, it was still summer and the sun went down very late, otherwise we would have had to deal with it in the pitch black when, at nearly ten o'clock at night, hours after we had been expecting them, the first car arrived – with four kids. Right behind it, in a convoy that ribboned down the street, more cars came. And more. And even bloody more. What the hell?

Father Neary popped out of one of the cars and came in to help put some order on the mishmash of people that were pouring through the doorway.

So far, I had seen ten children crossing my threshold and the cars kept arriving. The priest looked tired and dishevelled. He pulled me aside.

"Listen. I'm afraid there are a few more children than we thought. Things are very tough up there."

Kids were still filing in. Bloody hell – I counted thirteen now. I gulped.

"Alright, so. How many are we talking about?"

He fumbled with a piece of paper he had pulled out of his coat pocket.

"Em … *twirtle feeve.* "

He had mumbled that last bit pathetically.

"What? How many did you say?"

He cleared his throat.

"Now, we had only been expecting about a dozen, as you

know, but then the cars just kept showing up."

Out of the corner of my eye, I counted at least four more children. Doris was directing the flow like a traffic warden.

"And?"

"Em ... we have thirty-five. Altogether. Total."

At least he had the decency to look embarrassed.

"Jesus wept!" That was Doris. She made no apology to the priest for her outburst and, fair play to him, he didn't look offended.

"Alright, so." The children, some of them carrying small bags, some carrying a blanket, some with nothing at all, kept coming in. My own children were standing on the stairs, occasionally yelling helpful directions. "That's it, put your bag up on the table or the dog will get in it!"

"Where do we start?" Doris was trying to get everyone in one place, some of them had wandered into the back garden.

"Two things," I said. "Gwen and Rose, get your blankets, you'll be sleeping in the bath. Father, you and I need to go up and down the street and knock on some doors. We'll never get all this lot in here, we'll need some help."

So, that's what we did. I went to every single one of my neighbours and, God love them, at eleven o'clock at night, out of the clear blue, some of them opened their doors and found room for one or two. By the time we got back to my place, I only had to scrounge enough room for fifteen kids.

You do remember Father Neary saying that it would be just a day or two, right? A load of you-know-what, yet again. I had them for more than a week. They were aged from two to seventeen, some of them were siblings, some were alone and so frightened I don't know how they got through it. But, somehow, all of us, we managed.

Meals were done in shifts of six at a time. Even with all those hands to help, I was heartily sick of peeling potatoes! The washing machine ran constantly, but first we had to make sure that everyone labelled their clothes and their towels, if they had their own. We still had an occasional kerfuffle when someone decided they liked someone else's blouse better than their own – if the government up in the North was really serious about ending 'hostilities' they should have sent a platoon of teenage girls to sort it because there is very little that can stand up to that level of viciousness. We set up a chart with a rota of chores on it – for dishes, sweeping, taking out rubbish, minding younger ones, walking the dogs and on and on. One of the kids cheerfully – I hope! – nicknamed the place 'Camp Rio'.

Over the next week and a half, one-by-one, or two-by-two, Father Neary managed to find places for them. It was a relief and a disappointment at the same time. I found the house too quiet after they were all gone. The hustle and bustle had been exhausting, but also exhilarating.

I never again had that many children all at one time but, sad to say, that was only the beginning of the influx of the internment children. Over the next three years, I would continue to take them in, never more than a handful at a time, and serve as a sort of intermediary until either the Church or some other agency could find them something more permanent.

A lot of things I learned at that time stood me in good stead for later – putting name tags on the clothes, putting up a rota for the chores and for homework – these turned out to be good ways of keeping things running smoothly even when it wasn't like trying to organise a small army. As any mother can tell you, sometimes just trying to manage three or four kids can seem like a job for a field marshal.

∂❀❀∂

If she hadn't already been dying, I would have killed her.

I know my anger was misdirected, but I was so completely, unrestrainedly angry – at her, at God, at everything and everyone – because it seemed that they were all letting me down.

Doris had cancer. She had known for months and hadn't told me and she had only been given months to live.

She had wanted to 'spare' me, I suppose, and she had spent those months when she knew what was ahead of her, dealing with it alone. Maybe that's what hurt the most, that after everything we had shared, after being up to our noses in each other's business for so long, after she had been the only shoulder I had ever leaned on, that we had not shared this.

At the very end, she was in the hospital. By that time, all they could do was try and keep her pain bearable, though it was constant. I went to visit her as often as I could, though there was very little of her left to visit. She had been whittled down to a twig and the morphine kept her in a cloud of fuzzy memories and imagined landscapes. Sometimes she knew me. Most of the time she knew only the crazy meanderings that were going on in her head. I would sit by her all the same, no matter what she rambled and raved or mumbled about.

In those small spaces when she was quiet, I would talk to her about the old times. Retell stories of things we had done to remind her that she was a crazy, mad thing even back when she was well. She would like to remember that.

I tried, even then, to imagine what my life would be like without her. I couldn't. It was like trying to imagine that there was no sky. It was very much like knowing that there was no ground beneath my feet.

The day she died, I wasn't there. I had gone to attend some big family do – it had seemed important at the time. When I realised that she had passed over without me there to say goodbye, I didn't know what to do with myself. In all of my years, I had come across many grief-stricken people. I had always commiserated with their loss, how could you not? But, until the moment I lost Doris, I had not really *known* what that kind of grief felt like. I had not known that there could be such a complete, obliterating emptiness where my heart had been.

For Doris, at the end of her ordeal, they had been able to ease the pain that tormented her. But what was there for me? How was I supposed to make mine 'bearable'?

For the first few days I operated like a mechanical device – every day had its circumscribed chores that needed to be done, and that meant I didn't have to think about what to do, I could just do it. I had four children with me at the time – my own two, Rose, and a boy from Northern Ireland. The twin boys that had belonged to Doris had gone to live with a relative. They were teenagers by then and dealt with their grief with the resilience of youth. My own strength seemed to have deserted me. It had drained away, day by day, as I had sat next to her in that sterile hospital room. Now, I had nothing left and, in spite, of the people around me that depended on me and needed me, I felt as if I had no one, no one who would understand how lost I felt. Doris had been the only friend who had ever been there when I was hanging at the end of my tether. In a house full of people and a life that ran me ragged with places to go and things to do, I had never felt so alone.

The bustle of the daily run-around kept me functioning while the kids needed me but, at night, the pain would set in, full-blown and hungry. I would lie down and close my eyes and the tears would start without any let-up. Instead of sleep and dreams, I spent hours wracked with sobbing and would get up in the morning puffy-eyed and irritable, nearly insane with grief and guilt.

At first, the kids tiptoed around me, knowing that I was keeping up a fragile façade. But, of course, they healed faster than I ever could and the forward momentum of their lives carried them through. They would not have understood that I was still stuck in my own private mire of heartbreak. For their sakes, I managed to act as if I had also moved on but it got harder and harder as the days went by and I was still unable to rest. I started to get forgetful, my temper became so brittle that no one knew what would set me off into a tirade. Something big like a broken window, I would shrug off. A shoe at the bottom of the stairs might send me into an incandescent fury. I knew I was losing it.

I tried getting out of the house at night, which helped a little. I would go to wherever there was some music and sit through an evening of songs and chatting. Mind you, sitting there with the gang, there was no escaping the empty place where Doris had been. I knew they all felt it keenly as well but it was also understood that we could not wallow in our loss, that we had to consecrate her death with the perseverance of life. So, the singing was perhaps a bit more exuberant than before. The laughter more sharply edged. The conversation more fervent. I never forgot for a moment how much I was missing her, but the edge of my pain was dulled somewhat.

And it was there, among my friends, that I found my salvation and my damnation. I discovered drink.

Now, I had always enjoyed a jar or two when I was out and about, just like everyone did. The thing that made it different now was that, before, I had never *needed* to drink. I had indulged many times in beer and wine, and of course my exploits with poitín were legendary, but I had always been able to take it or leave it. I had never thought of it as a place to hide. But, one night, when my heart felt like a stone, someone introduced me to brandy and in its warm fire I found that I could finally drink enough to shut up the demons in my head. I could crawl into a dark, empty place and find, if not sleep, then an unconsciousness that at least allowed me to rest.

At first, it was just occasional – just on those nights when I knew I was approaching a meltdown – that I learned how to drink myself into a tipsy, mindless state. Everything would get pleasantly fuzzy and the jagged edges of my memories were blunted. It was just enough that I could still manage to get myself home, but I remained fuzzy enough that I would collapse on my bed and remain blissfully semi-conscious until I had to get up and get the kids sorted. I convinced myself that they never noticed if I was a little the worse for wear.

Obviously, I couldn't go out every night and, eventually, just escaping on those nights when I could get away was not enough. I had to find a way to kill the pain on the nights when I stayed at home, too. That was when brandy came home with me so that I could crawl inside it every night.

I developed a new routine. At the end of the long day, after getting all of the kids and the husband sorted, I would turn down all of the lights in the house except for one in the kitchen. I would switch on the radio or the television, sit in my comfortable chair and start sipping my brandy. At first, I would sit and sip until I felt the heavy claws of pain stop raking across my heart. Then, as soon as I felt that I could slip into a pain-free haze, I would shift myself up the stairs and into my bed.

Gradually, as time went on, just sipping a glass or two until the pain was dulled was not enough. It needed to be erased. It needed to be expunged. So, the drinking would go on until I was unconscious, right there in my chair. For a good while I was able to wake myself up before the children came down, so that they didn't know that I hadn't made it to bed. But, eventually, there came those mornings when they would find me, sloppily snoring in the chair, still in my clothes from the day before.

I don't know how long this could have gone on. If everything hadn't gone to hell, perhaps I would still be drinking myself senseless today – because, God knows, I still miss Doris now as much as I did back then. I wasn't really living, I was surviving by day and killing myself by night. I convinced myself that I was coping and that no one was suffering, but God and his angels knew that I was crawling into a pit that was going to swallow me whole, so, they sent me a message.

Going out for the music and the fun was getting sloppier and sloppier. There were mornings when I couldn't remember what I had done the night before. When my friends would tell me, it would be funny – or embarrassing. Then there started to be the mornings when I couldn't remember coming home. I couldn't remember driving, I couldn't remember coming through the door. Eventually, there were mornings when I awoke to discover I hadn't made it to my bed – I had come in the door and collapsed on the sofa. Or the floor.

Eventually, came the morning when I nearly died.

I still don't know what was different about that night – who I was with, how much I drank, why I was so out of my mind – but I drove myself home and that is a thought that frightens me to this day. The state I must have been in.

I awoke, bleary-eyed, cramped, cold and with a mouth that tasted like I had swallowed an old pair of socks. As I looked around, I couldn't believe it. It was in the early stages of daylight and I was lying, curled up, on the grass in front of my doorstep. My car was next to me, the driver's side door still ajar.

I began to panic. Had I hit something? I could have hit all kinds of things on my way home – had I hit a tree? Had I hit another car? My God, had I hit a person? A child? I started to feel sick. I couldn't remember anything about driving home. Nothing.

It was difficult to stand up straight but I managed to clamber up and inspect the car. There wasn't a mark on it that I could see and the keys were still in the ignition. But my clothes felt strange, damp and clingy, as if I had been caught in the rain.

I checked myself in a clumsy, half drunken attempt to see what was what. It was a mess. I had vomited on myself. And I had wet myself, too.

I sat down on the step and collapsed, then I bent over and gave in to a choking, gasping sob. I let myself cry, letting go of all the bruising sorrow I had been holding back for so long, letting loose the flood of tears I had been trying to dam up with the alcohol.

I spent a few moments gathering myself then grabbed my keys and let myself into the house. Keeping as quiet as I could, I took a shower in water as hot as I could stand. Then I came downstairs and fixed myself a pot of coffee. I drank the whole thing, one mug at a time. When I started to retch, I just poured myself another cup and made myself drink it.

Still as quiet as I could be, I got back into the car and drove. I knew exactly where I needed to go.

I arrived at Mount Argus just as the morning traffic was getting into full swing. The doors to the church weren't open, so I went to the reception desk at the monastery and told the brother there that I wanted to take the pledge.

He didn't even blink. He just looked me in the eye, nodded, and took me into a small waiting room. A few minutes later, a priest came in. We talked for a few minutes, I gave him a brief summary of what I had been through and what I had done, and then, with a rosary in one hand and my other on the Bible, I took the pledge – I swore to God and heaven and all the angels and anyone else who might be listening – that I would never drink another drop of alcohol for the rest of my life.

The priest was a kindly, old man. He took my hand when we were done and he said, "You do know that this is just the start. Now you need to heal the wound that made you drink in the first place." He handed me a card for a psychiatric counsellor.

I took the card, fully intending to throw it away. In all my life up to that point, I had never had a good opinion about counsellors or psychologists or therapists or any analysts who wanted to get inside somebody's head. I had known people who had gone through various types of therapies and spent years sitting on someone's couch yarning on and on about their childhood. I thought it was a load of worthless rubbish.

However, that night the longing for the drink was like a burning oil on my soul. When the following morning finally came, I knew I wasn't going to be able to keep my pledge without some help. So, I called the lady whose name was on the card, Ruth.

To be honest, the first few meetings were just as painful as not drinking. I was beginning to despair that it was ever going to be worthwhile, and every day I was in agony, not knowing what was more terrifying – having another drink, or never having one ever again. I don't know exactly what the breakthrough was, but somehow Ruth pried something open and all of the pain that I had been forcing out of sight broke free and slapped me right in the face. I thought I had been broken by grief but, at that moment, I realised that I had, in fact, been destroyed by my refusal to face it. I needed to learn to live with my broken heart and stop retreating from it. There was nowhere to hide that would ever be safe. There was nothing in the bottle that would ever save me, that would ever be my friend, that would ever bring any kind of help or healing. I would have to find all of those things within myself.

In short, Ruth made me face my loss and she saved my life. Some day, it will be my turn to pass over to the other side and I know Doris will be there waiting for me. And, I still say that the first thing I will do is box her ears for putting me through all of this. God love her.

Meanwhile, I don't have time to wallow in it. There's a lot to be done and I need to get to it.

Epilogue

The Beginning

Father Neary walked up the footpath towards the white door. There was a basket of bright flowers hanging near the doorbell and a small statue of an angel (*Or is it a fairy?* he thought, with a smile) on the doorstep. The whole yard was swept tidy and he could hear the snap of clean laundry hanging on the line around the back. Behind the door he could hear the thumping of at least two pairs of feet galloping down the stairs followed by some childish shouts and chatter.

Such a homely, welcoming place. Such a delight and comfort after the nightmare he had faced all afternoon.

He pressed the doorbell and braced himself.

The door was opened by a lad of about eight. He was still in school uniform, though his tie was askew and his shirt-tail was hanging out below his jumper. He had a red lollipop in his hand.

He looked at the priest and waved the lolly.

"Hi ya there, Father."

"Hello, Thomas. Is she in?"

"Sure she is. Come on in." He pushed the door open. As Father Neary crossed the threshold, Thomas waved the lolly in his direction. "Would you like one? We have more. The red ones are the best."

"No thank you, Thomas, but you are very kind to ask."

Father Neary followed him down the short hallway to the kitchen.

It was like entering a beehive.

Pots were burbling away on the stove, simmering with smells of potatoes and broccoli. There were two children seated at the kitchen table, schoolbooks and papers and pencils and crayons scattered about. They were jabbering and flipping pages and papers. Two posters on the brightly painted wall displayed addition and multiplication tables. Shelves around the room held figurines of angels and fairies and butterflies. He heard more children outside in the garden, kicking a football. A dog was barking.

Herself was at the sink, water was running; she was cleaning a couple of chickens for roasting. She peered at him over the top of her glasses.

"How are ya there, Father?"

"Very well, Rio, very well. And yourself?"

"Can't complain. Sure you'll have a cuppa tea? Gwen put the kettle on will ya, there's a good girl."

"No, no. I won't be here long. I just need to ask you for something."

Rio pulled the chickens out of the sink and placed them in a roasting pan.

"Oh no you don't." She gave him a grin. "Look at the state of the place. Five is all I can handle at the moment."

"Of course, of course. No, I'm not asking you to take on any more children – I know your hands are full. But I could use your help, all the same."

She was rubbing the chickens with salt and pepper and looking over at the kitchen table.

"Rose! Don't use your crayons for your homework! Use your pencil."

She turned back to the priest.

"And what is it that I can help you with, Father?"

"It's a family that needs your help – and you'd be helping them and me both. It would be in a sort of formal capacity."

"Formal?" She snorted. "Whatever that means."

She placed the roasting pan in the oven and checked the potatoes.

"I can't take in any more children right now, just so's you know."

"Yes, I understand." Father Neary had to step to one side as Thomas came tearing through the kitchen and nearly knocked him sideways. "I want you to help some of the mothers."

Rio's eyebrows went up as she wiped her hands on a towel.

"The mothers?"

"Yes, I have some families that are struggling and they just need someone like yourself to come in and help them organise their homes. Someone who can come in and help them cope with a houseful of children and the laundry and the school work." He waved his hand around the kitchen.

"We have some poor mothers that will lose their children to foster care if they don't get a grip on how to deal with things. We're looking for folks, such as yourself, to come out to them two or three times a week and just help them get organised. We're calling them 'visiting home workers'."

She grinned at that.

"Now, look at me, Father. I'm up to my nose in 'homework'."

He smiled. "Rio, ever since you helped with the children from the North, I've known that you have a special gift. Some of these women have seven, or ten, even fifteen children of their own and they don't have a clue how to manage. Everyone in the family suffers as a result."

Rio suddenly tapped a wooden spoon on the window. "Patrick, put that down! And give Christy back his shoe!"

She turned to Father Neary.

"Well, I can only come in and tell them what I do. I don't even know if it's right or it's wrong, I just know that it works for me. Mostly."

"That's it exactly. I have a family nearby that I'm working with right now. Will you come with me tomorrow for a quick visit just to see if there is anything you can do?"

"Gwen, be a good girl and see if those clothes on the line are dry, will you?" She turned to the priest and pushed her glasses up a bit. "Well, I can pop in for a visit and see if there is anything I can do to help. I can't promise I can do it full-time, like."

"Oh, no problem, that's grand. I'll collect you at ten tomorrow morning – will that suit?"

"Alright, so."

"I'll see myself out. Thanks a million, Rio. See you tomorrow."

He turned to go.

"Father!"

"Yes?"

"I'm not bringing home any more kids!"

"I know, I know. Thanks, Rio. See you tomorrow."

He closed the kitchen door behind him. As he stepped outside, he leaned over and touched the head of the angel on the doorstep.

"Thanks," he whispered.

The next day, Father Neary collected Rio and they drove to a treeless area of council flats. The family they were visiting consisted of a mother and father and seven children, with an eighth child on the way. They were squashed into a flat that was far too small for them. He explained that he was desperately trying to sort out better accommodation for them but that, in the meantime, they needed to get their current living situation under some kind of control.

The outside of the building looked like most buildings of the sort. Ugly, square architecture. Oddments of rubbish were scattered here and there, bicycles in various states of repair, random piles of dog dirt. They climbed the stairs to the second floor.

"This is it." Father Neary hesitated a moment. "Em, I guess I should warn you..."

"Warn me? You're gonna warn me now, while we're on the bleedin' doorstep?"

"Sorry, but ... well, things here are a bit rough. Just remember, that's why they need your help."

He knocked on the door. For a moment after it opened, Rio did not see the girl who stood in the doorway. It felt as if her head had been buffeted by the plume of stale, wretched air that escaped out through the door frame.

As Father Neary stepped in, the assault escalated. Little hands grabbed at his legs and arms. He laughed and gave each little hand a squeeze. All four of them were yelling at the top of their voices.

"Sweets! Where's the sweets!"

He stopped and reached into his coat pocket.

"Why, I just might have some right here." He stopped for a moment and looked perplexed. "Oh dear, I hope I didn't forget them!"

There was a huge flood of moans and groans.

A little boy, who looked to be about five, piped up with, "You better not have forgot, ya poxy bastard."

Rio nearly swallowed her teeth.

"Now then, we won't be having that kind of language." She pointed her fiercest mum-glare at him through her glasses. The tyke responded by kicking her in the shins.

"Jesus!" She reached down and rubbed her leg. The boy stuck his tongue out at her, shoved one of his smaller siblings out of the way, and grabbed at the priest's arm.

"Ya got any or not!"

The priest took a step forward so that they could close the

door.

"Alright, alright. I was just teasing you, children, here are some sweets now."

He pulled a handful of wrapped sweets out of his pocket and held them out. The result was similar to a feeding frenzy Rio had once seen on a television nature programme about wildebeests.

While the children were occupied, Rio took a look around the room. It was a cramped space, made more cramped by the accumulation of random bits and pieces of unrecognisable junk – there even looked to be pieces of a dismantled car engine sitting in a corner – piles of clothing and blankets that did not look likely to be clean, rumpled sheets of wet newspaper scattered about and, at the end of the room, in the corner, was what appeared to be the kitchen. There were chairs and a table – littered with dirty plates and cutlery – crusty pans and cooking utensils, assorted crumpled bags and wrappings. Some flies were wafting lazily around, most were crawling undisturbed across the layers of grease and the carpet of crumbs that served as a tabletop.

Next to the sagging sofa was an accumulation of cardboard boxes and dingy, dismally ragged pillows stacked in a crude semi-circle. Rio could see a ginger head of curls behind it. She walked over and found a girl, aged about a year and a half, penned up in the roughly organised containment area. She wore a filthy tee-shirt that was too small for her, and nothing else. There had been an attempt to cover the small bit of floor beneath her with newspaper. It was wet, shredded in places and smeared with a greenish brown slime. She was lying on her side, looking towards Rio. The only noise she made was a wheezing sound, her tiny chest trembling with the exertion of each breath. She did not make any noise and did not move. Only her eyes followed Rio as she came closer.

Father Neary came up behind her.

"That's Lily, she's the youngest. She's had some kind of lung condition since she was born. I think I told you there is another one on the way."

"Where's the mother?" Rio had to clench her jaw to keep from screaming. Her hands were shaking and she half hoped that the mother wasn't there, as she might be tempted to tear the woman's head off if she got within two feet of her.

The priest turned to the girl who had opened the door.

"Would you go and get your mammy?"

She furrowed her brow and pushed her hair behind her ears. Her younger brothers and sisters were scrabbling around on the floor looking for a sweet that someone thought they might have dropped.

"Mammy's resting. She doesn't like to be bothered when she's resting."

"It's okay, love." Rio tried to smile. It was like trying to swim through plaster. "She'll want to see the Father now, won't she?"

The girl didn't seem at all sure, but she ran towards the back of the flat, knocked on a door and slipped inside the room.

The priest turned to Rio.

"It may take a few minutes for her to get up and come out here."

"Well, then I'll have a good look around, shall I? Get an idea of what needs to be done."

She had already determined that there were no nappies for the littlest ones – that was the reason for the newspaper all over the floor. She poked her head into a door off to the left of the front room and found a bathroom – there was no hot water at the tap. The smell had been a fair warning but she decided to be thorough and lifted the toilet lid. It was backed up with solid matter that gave off a reek that would have choked the devil. She dropped the lid, gagging, and immediately ran her hands under the cold water in the sink. She looked for soap. Or a towel: There was just the ubiquitous newspaper along with some soiled clothing and even dirty dishes.

In the kitchen, she poked around in the presses, hoping to find food. There was a box of Weetabix with not much more than crumbs at the bottom. Some grubby plastic cups, a box of tea bags and several small bottles of vodka. There were hard, crusty piles of dark matter scattered here and there on the shelves. Mouse droppings, probably.

The fridge was a tiny thing on the floor, stuck crookedly into a corner. She opened it and was greeted by a waft of warm, swampy air that smelled of fungus. The boy who had kicked her was behind her.

"That don't work."

"Yes, I see that."

"We keeps the milk and butter in the sink. Ya can put cold water on it, see."

He went to the sink and pulled up a small bottle of milk that was just a quarter full.

Rio took it from his small hands. It was tepid. She looked in the sink and the only thing there, floating in a puddle of water, was a small plastic tub of margarine.

"That's very good – thanks for showing me that. Is it alright if I look at a few more things around here?"

The boy shrugged and started to pick his nose, but continued to watch her carefully.

Rio poked through the piles of dishes and pots then opened another press, below the sink. This was, apparently, where they had been putting their rubbish. There was a plastic pail that had been filled with food scraps and dirtied bits of newspaper, food wrappers and empty tins – and it was roiling with a lively population of maggots.

Rio slammed the cupboard door shut.

When she stood, she leaned on the sink and closed her eyes, squeezing her mouth closed so that the children would not see her fighting the bile rising in her throat.

She heard footsteps and voices behind her. Rio didn't know what to expect when she turned around – she didn't know what kind of demon the woman in charge of this household would turn out to be. A huge, vicious, alcoholic with rotten teeth perhaps. Or a shrill, demanding harridan with a wicked temper. Anyone who raised a family in this manner must surely be a decayed husk of misplaced humanity.

Rio turned and saw Father Neary with a small, fragile-looking woman, with a bird-like delicacy of bone and movement. Her once-blonde hair was a drab, greyish yellow, pulled back in an elastic band. Her pregnant belly looked like a disfigurement, a grotesque growth completely out of proportion to her frailty. Her face was youngish, near to forty, but her eyes were lined with an age that had nothing to do with years. She moved hesitantly. The children crowded around her and she held out a hand to ward them off.

"Watch it there! Don't knock me over! Who's watching Lily?" Her voice was surprisingly strong and rough, an incongruous mismatch with her slender lightness.

The kids all babbled at once then the oldest one made a beeline for the stack of pillows that served as Lily's playpen. Her bed, too, most likely.

"Rio, this is Maddy, mother of this brood."

Rio put out her hand.

"Nice to meet ya."

Maddy didn't smile. She didn't seem surly or unfriendly, she seemed numb.

"Well, yas can all sit down." And she sat down in a chair furthest from the window.

Rio kept quiet as Father Neary and Maddy discussed things; she kept her eyes on the kids at times, on Maddy at other times, listening, taking in the story of how this family had come to be, as the story fleshed itself out.

The father was rarely at home, but he was around. He seemed to be the sort who was always dabbling in money-making notions, such as engine repair, but wouldn't stay sober or interested long enough for anything to pan out. The dole money seemed to disappear like breath on a glass and they were always short of everything. Maddy couldn't answer for where the money went, she didn't get to see much of it herself. She suspected that he did some betting as well as drinking but would never dream of confronting him. It seemed to take all of her energy to ask for milk money for the children.

Because Maddy was not feeling well with this pregnancy, the kids were not going to school regularly – there were many mornings when she just couldn't get up. The two youngest children, Lily and a boy who was three, had never been potty trained. The toilet only worked occasionally and Maddy had run out of the stamina and concentration needed to train the kids to do more than aim for the ever-present newspaper. Meal times were unorganised, random, sometimes completely missed; shopping was chaotic.

Everything in the household reeked of abandonment. Maddy had abandoned all hope of having any control over her choices, her surroundings or the trajectory of her life. The father was both the abandoner and the abandoned – adrift in a miasma of drink, aimlessness and unfocused rage. The children bore the brunt of the abandonment, eking out an existence, half-starved for both love and sustenance.

Rio felt ridiculous. How could the priest have thought that she could come in here with her shopping lists and laundry rota and homework schedule and make any kind of difference in their lives? She had never felt so overwhelmed. For the first time in her life, she felt inadequate.

When their visit was over, Rio and Father Neary said their goodbyes. A couple of the children had gone outside, the remaining ones clung to the priest as he was trying to leave. They begged for more sweets, they begged for a cruise around the neighbourhood in his car, they begged to be taken down to the shop, they begged, they begged, they begged. Maddy sat, dry eyed and unsmiling on the chair where they left her, her hand on her distended belly, clenched in a white-knuckled fist.

The fresh air outside the door slapped Rio in the face. She shuddered with the cold delight of it, shaking off the fug of what they had left behind. Yet, the leaving had torn at her. *How can I leave them here?* she thought, *And how will I ever be able to come back?*

They walked down the flights of stairs in silence. Halfway down, Rio lurched to the railing and surrendered to the clawing nausea that had been stalking her for what seemed like hours now. She vomited over the railing quickly, furiously.

Wiping her mouth she staggered back and Father Neary patted her shoulder.

"I know, I know," he was murmuring. "It's very difficult, it breaks the heart … I know."

Rio pulled a tissue from her pocket and dabbed at her lips. Tears were dripping down as well.

"Jesus, Mary and Joseph!" She glared at him over the top of her glasses. "Pardon my language, Father, but what in the name of heaven have you gotten me into?"

His smile was tired.

"I wonder myself, Rio. This is all new territory. We'll have to figure it out as we go, I'm afraid."

They continued down the stairs. The drive home was fairly short and Rio was unusually quiet. Father Neary tried to get her to talk about it – he explained all about how he was going to do things, all the plans he had for helping families like Maddy's, he told her that the home workers would do so much more than the Church and the charities had ever been able to – but she would not be drawn into a conversation.

After they stopped in her drive, Rio sat for a moment.

"So, what do we do next, Father?"

"Ah, so you want to help, do you? That's great to hear."

"There is nothing in this world I would rather *not* do but you know, as well as I do, that I can't just walk away from it. So, where do I start?"

"Could you come along tomorrow? Yourself and another home worker can help them start cleaning the place up? I'll be sorting some things with a social worker."

"Fair enough, I can do that." She opened the door and got out. Before she pushed the car door shut, she turned to the priest.

"But I won't be bringing home any more children. Is that clear? I won't be having any social workers or this one and that one putting their noses into my business."

He nodded. "I understand. Anything you can do to help is very much appreciated, you know that."

"Alright." And she shut the door.

Over the next few weeks, Rio made several trips to the flat, along with another home worker named Helen. They spent hours sorting through rubbish, showing the kids how to sweep and dust and mop; scrubbing floors and toilets, sinks and dishes. Laundry had to be dealt with. Shopping lists had to be worked out. A schedule for getting the kids up and off to school was arranged.

Through it all, Maddy stayed distant and uninterested, the father nearly invisible – except to burst in and throw a tantrum. They found a used playpen for Lily and Rio tried to get Maddy involved in bathing Lily and playing with her. The toddler had been struggling with lung problems since she was born and was supposed to be taking medication. A social worker and a home nurse got that sorted, so Rio helped train Maddy in how to give Lily her medicine and how to give the breathing therapy that she needed. But even this failed to engage her – Maddy stayed distant and removed.

For Rio, the sessions with Lily were the only part of the visit where she felt that she had accomplished something. Lily had been a scarily quiet child at first, but, as the days passed, she got more energetic, more playful. She only said a few words, but it was clear she was bright enough to learn more. She needed time, Rio knew. Time to heal, time to get stronger. But the nurse had warned Rio that if the medication wasn't given regularly and if the therapy didn't progress, time was not an option. Maddy seemed unable, or unwilling, to help Lily fight for her little life. Rio had to do all the fighting and it was wearing her down.

On many days, Rio and Helen would turn up and Maddy would stay in bed. Everything that Rio and Helen got sorted would get undone either by the children, who slipped back into their chaotic ways as soon as they were left alone, or by their father, drunk and belligerent, determined to get the priest and the home workers out of his way.

The nurse called in once a week to check on Maddy's pregnancy. Maddy was meant to be taking vitamins and getting out of bed more. Instead, she seemed to be slipping away, receding further and further, circumscribed by a world consisting of her darkened room and a cocoon of musty blankets. It was the only space she cared to inhabit. She did not care to eat, she did not tolerate, let alone enjoy, the company of any of her children. They were losing her.

She was eight months pregnant when she woke in the middle of the night, aware of the violent kicking inside her. She wanted to scream and was afraid that the three younger children sleeping in the room with her would hear her thrashing around. In the weeks and months before, all she had wanted was to stay under her blankets, with the curtains closed, the bedroom door shut. She had wanted to keep her eyes away from the light that dissolved her dreams. Now, persistent, writhing torsions were slamming against the inside of the skin of her belly and made her want nothing more than to get up into the hostile air. The room that had been her refuge now seemed to be smothering her and she needed to get out, out, out.

She pulled the blanket up around her shoulders and hobbled to the toilet, quietly, slipping on bare feet, biting her tongue. She staggered into the tiny tiled room and turned on the light. No, no, no, this wouldn't do either. She padded into the front room, afraid that the kicking inside her was making such a thunderous noise that it would wake up the children scattered on the cushions.

When they did not stir, she carefully pulled the front door open. It was raining and, for the first time in years, she relished the wetness and the cold, opened her mouth and let the drops slap against her tongue. *Yes, we need to take a walk, that's why you're kicking – you want to stretch your legs.*

She dropped the blanket behind her and stepped out into the night.

It was very early in the morning when Rio's doorbell rang.

She was already up. Padding about in her dressing gown and

slippers in the kitchen, she had been getting out loaves of bread and packages of ham for the children to make their sandwiches to take to school.

She opened the door, expecting the bin man or some such, not Father Neary.

His face looked grey, the lines around his mouth deeper.

"Jesus, Father, you're a fright! Begging your pardon, now do come in."

He came into the hall and stopped.

"Rio, can you get away and come to Maddy's? Someone needs to stay with the children for a bit."

"Well, of course. What's happened?"

"The baby."

"Ah, Jesus. Oh, sorry again, Father. The poor dear is early!"

Before Father Neary could answer, Rio was putting on her coat and calling up the stairs.

"Gwen! Come down here, love, I need your help."

She turned back to the priest.

"Now, let me get my handbag … my goodness, I'm not ready for this at all. She's at the hospital, I take it?"

"Yes … she's not well, I'm afraid."

He had given this kind of news before. He waited.

"Oh, no! What's wrong?"

Father Neary heard some footsteps upstairs. He had to make this quick.

"She wandered off last night in that storm – they found her this morning, wracked with a fever. She lost the baby."

Today was a day when there should have been rain.

It seemed to Rio that the heavens should have been pouring,

though whether to mourn or to purge, she wasn't sure.

At the least there should have been grey skies. The emptiness above their heads should have been dark, oppressive and bleak. The crystal blueness and optimistic sunshine of that winter day was breaking her heart.

Father Neary's car drove through the busy streets towards Maddy's flat and Rio blinked at the bright blur of colours as people flittered about, doing all of the mundane things of their lives as usual. If only, she thought. If only we could go back to life as usual.

When they arrived, a social worker and a nurse were there. The children were in the front room, oddly subdued. Voices rose and fell from the bedroom at the back. Rio couldn't make out what they were saying, but it seemed to be the usual roaring of Maddy's husband punctuated by the temperate voice of another social worker: She was trying to stem the flood of his drunken denial, and drowning.

Father Neary and the social worker immediately went into a huddle, she with a fistful of papers. Rio went to the children. Two of the smaller ones got up, let her sit down on the crowded sofa and then climbed on her lap. Ah, life as usual.

Rio had to blink for a moment and force a smile.

"So, has everyone had some breakfast? Do ya need anything?" There was some mumbling, some nodding. She looked around the crowded floor.

"Where is Lily?"

"A nurse has her. She was wheezing again. Did ya bring any sweets?"

Rio tousled the nearest head.

"Just could be that I did, love. How about if we take a look in my bag?"

There was so much milling about. The social workers and Father Neary were filling out papers, a Garda came and went, the nurse was popping around, to and fro. The children's father made an appearance, refused to sign something, made a fuss, got everyone upset. He disappeared, then came back – more amenable after having had a few pints of something. He finally did whatever it was they wanted him to do, but made sure he was surly about it. He left in an uproar, slamming the door behind him. He had never even looked at the children.

Rio had to make several trips getting kids to the toilet, getting glasses of water, making cups of tea, finding a lost shoe. But, compared to the rest of it, it seemed as if she and the children stayed still while all the milling went on around them. Finally, it was time. Father Neary had tried to prepare Rio, but there was nothing for it except to let it happen. He explained to the children that they would be going to foster homes. Three children were going to one home and three to another.

At first, they just looked at him as if he had spoken Greek. They had no idea what a foster home was.

"You're going to go and live with other families for a while." Rio hoped that she sounded cheerful. She was trying. Trying so hard.

The eldest girl had copped on first.

"But why? Why can't we stay with our own ma?"

"Now, you know your ma is in the hospital. This is just until she is well enough that you can come home again."

"Bollocks!" That was the five-year-old. "I doesn't want to go nowhere."

Father Neary stooped down to look the youngest ones in the eyes.

"I know this seems a bit scary, but you'll be somewhere where you get lots to eat and have your own bed and everything."

As these were all things completely out of their experience, they just looked back at him blankly. One little girl hiccupped.

"And, you can all come and visit me whenever you like." Rio nearly bit her own tongue off after she realised what she had said, but there it was, she had said it.

A couple of the older children smiled a bit at that. The younger ones still did not know what to think.

Their belongings were gathered, coats and hats were scrounged, a sort of order was imposed and the social worker got them ready to take them to their new homes.

Rio hugged each of them goodbye, gave each a sweet, kept her eyes dry for their sakes.

Then they were gone. An entire family of children, dispersed like so many loaves of bread. But only six of them.

"Where is Lily?"

Father Neary looked as tired as she had ever seen him. "She's still in the bedroom with the nurse."

"Why didn't she go to a home with some of her brothers and sisters?"

He sat down, and Rio realised he was shaking a bit.

"She can't go to a foster home, Rio. We don't have any foster parents who are prepared to deal with a child with such a serious illness. She'll go to an orphanage."

It was a relief to finally have somewhere to spend her anger. It came with a volcanic urgency.

"An orphanage for that poor little thing? After all that this family has been through? She bloody well will NOT go to an orphanage. Over my fucking dead body!"

She didn't care any more that she was talking to a priest. A stream of language that she normally reserved for bad drivers and corrupt politicians thundered around her as she stormed back to the bedroom. The nurse had laid Lily on the bed, on her side, where she lay pathetically still, her chest rising and falling with soft wheezing sounds. The nurse was sorting through Lily's medications – a small satchel was already packed with her few clothes and a ragged pillow that she liked.

When Rio walked in, Lily lifted her head a little and smiled, reached out an arm. Rio leaned down and picked her up without thinking, her grip gentle but fierce. The nurse turned to look at her, but said nothing. Father Neary came through the door directly behind her.

"Now, Rio, you know it's best. No one knows better than yourself the amount of help this child needs."

"That's the first smart thing you've said! She certainly needs better than she'll get in some bloody orphanage. She needs more than medicine and therapy, and you know it – this child needs *care*. Real honest-to-God *care*."

Her face was wet, her glasses slippery against her face. She had held the tears back for so long, it seemed like forever. Now, there was nowhere else for them to go, the torrent had started. Father Neary stepped closer.

"Rio, she either goes into the foster care programme with

someone who can care for her, or she goes to the orphanage. There are no other choices."

She glared at him, though the look's usual effectiveness was ruined by the globs of tears, and her need to give a big sniff. The nurse came up to her, arms out, as if to take Lily away.

Rio felt the rattling in Lily's chest as she held her close. She looked down and saw the small mouth curl slightly upward in a lazy smile, the lips tinged with blue. Lily's brown eyes gazed back at Rio, earnest and unblinking.

"Alright, give me your poxy papers and I'll fill them out." She turned to the nurse and gave her the full force of her over-the-top-of-the-glasses glare. "And you give me that damned satchel."

She shifted Lily to her shoulder and patted her back.

"I'm taking this child home."